**REAL
ESTATE**
ROOKIE

THE HANDBOOK

FOR **BRAND NEW**

REAL ESTATE

AGENTS

REAL ESTATE ROOKIE

STEVE CONDURELIS, BROKER

Real Estate Rookie: The Handbook for Brand New Real Estate Agents

For information about this title or to order other books
and/or electronic media, contact the publisher:

Pipeline Publishers, LLC
Pipelinepublisher.com
Steve@pipelinepublisher.com

ISBNs:
978-1-63684-483-1 (softcover)
978-1-63684-482-4 (eBook)

Cover and Interior design: 1106 Design

This book is dedicated to the men and women of the Army, Navy, Marines, and Air Force who have dedicated their lives to the defense of our country. They sacrificed part of their life (or all of it) for us. Hopefully, this book will serve as a jump-start into a new and wonderful career.

Contents

Preface

Forty or so years ago I worked in corporate real estate. I was young, single, and traveled every week to a new city. My job was to advise and sell wealthy clients determined to avoid paying taxes. The work was stimulating, profitable, and fun. Our company delivered our products beautifully. Year after year we set growth and sales records. We grew into one of the premier companies in our industry. I enjoyed a decent salary and commission. Life was good.

The family company I worked for had been in business for 40+ years and never lost a dime for its clients. Clients lined up to use our services and buy our products.

Then came the crash. Congress called it the Tax act of 1986. Overnight the U.S. commercial real estate market collapsed. Billions of dollars of real estate value virtually evaporated. Thousands of people were laid off. Our company (along with its' unblemished history of profits), declared bankruptcy and ultimately liquidated.

I was now out of a job and on the street. I was determined to remain in commercial real estate and take full advantage of my excellent training. The interviews were few and far between. I found myself competing with people that had MBA's and multiple years of experience. My undergrad degree and relatively few years of experience could not compete.

The only industry that seemed to offer some hope was the residential sales business. There were only a few issues: The business was 100% commission based. There was no salary, no per diem, and no bonus structure. Dang, I was used to making good money. Life had been fun and interesting prior to this. I had always worked for a good salary. Residential home sales offered nothing like that.

Preliminary research on the local residential real estate market yielded even more disheartening information. Interest rates hovered at 12%. The housing industry had drifted into a coma. I discovered that the very best agents in our market had sold only one or two homes in the past year. Hundreds of real estate agents in our market retired or quit. The future prospects were bleak.

Taking an unemployment check was out of the question. That's not the way I was raised. Obviously the necessity to survive became very real and present in my life. I made the only decision I could, I went looking for a residential broker to work with.

Following a series of interviews, I was hired by a local leading luxury real estate firm. The owner was a one man show. He had worked in a "MLS free" environment his entire four decade long career. Please note that there was an MLS at the time, he just chose to not use it. He felt he didn't need it. He didn't. He was so good he literally "owned" the upscale market. He had become so entrenched and so highly skilled that no agent could challenge him. Wealthy clients only trusted his contacts and his expertise. Realizing this about him, I figured he had a bit of time left and certainly the experience to show me the ropes. He hired me as his flunky and promised to train me.

I did not realize it at the time, but I had wandered into a vast sea of knowledge and wisdom. Over the few years I worked with him I learned to pay very close attention to his coaching. I discovered his "good ole boy Southern manner" was comforting and welcoming to his clients. He was a thoroughly relaxed, confident and mature agent. He was in fact the consummate professional. He always took me to all his new listings. Each home tour included a tutorial on how to spot quality home construction and poor-quality home construction.

I could not get enough of his wisdom. I witnessed his masterful guidance of his clients into sales or purchases they ultimately **loved**. He was a magician!

He taught me that asking questions of my clients and listening intently to their responses was the golden key to his success. Yes sir, I had unknowingly stumbled into a grand wealth of knowledge.

Regardless of his fine training it still took eighteen months to sell my first home. The time he spent training me was finally paying off.

Then life delivered another surprise. Out of the blue, my mentor announced his retirement, along with the closing of his company. He wasn't going to sell it, give it away, or merge with anyone. He was going to simply close it. In just a few weeks, he walked out of the office, cut off the lights, locked the door, and never returned. He even left his furniture.

Back on the street again.

I joined another "up and coming" firm in our luxury market. They ushered me to the bull pen. "Here you go, come to me with any questions". No formal training. A phone, a desk, and the yellow pages. You sell or you starve. I was just another cog in the wheel, nothing special. It became patently clear that my success or failure was completely up to me. Like many real estate agents, working without a net became the key to my success. There was no other way.

With no past clients (or reputation as a local residential sales expert), I began my next new job by holding other agents open houses. Excellent! This would be my chance to get to know possible buyers or sellers and find ways to help them.

As one would expect, open house attendance was nearly non-existent. The hours were long, lonely, silent, and scary.

My checking account had dwindled to almost zero. My savings were gone. I was into the last drops of my retirement account.

Desperation was setting in. "Ah ha!"! I had forgotten about my change jar in the closet! Quarters first, then dimes, then nickels. I lived off the quarters at first, then the dimes, and then the nickels.

Then it happened. I was desperate for a sale. While holding an open house one Sunday, a lovely young couple did in fact wander in. They showed some interest my listing. Wonder of wonders.

Their initial interest extended into thirty minutes and edged into almost an hour. Finally, I asked them, "I hope you will forgive me, but I have left you guys alone to explore and enjoy this home on your own. I'm sure you must have some questions." They asked some pertinent questions that I was prepared to answer. Then, it just came out of my mouth, "I can tell you guys love this home." "Why don't you just buy it?" The husband and wife looked at each other and then agreed with me. They wanted the home.

They said yes! What? I was dumfounded.

I had done it and didn't realize it, I had asked the worlds simplest question and received the answer I was not expecting, "Yes".

We wrote an offer and thirty days later, the sale closed.

It was a big-ticket sale and a decent commission. I was out of the economic basement for a few months. Most importantly, I had learned a lesson I have never forgotten. I had finally learned to ask the worlds simplest question! "Would you like to buy it?"

I also learned that I was in need of more education. It was the 1980's and the internet had not been invented. Off to the bookstore I went. I bought one book at a time. Since open houses were rarely busy, I read my new books.

Two more dreary years drug by. I lived like a monk and kept spending my money and time in a deep study of the industry. Sales came, but slowly. Finally, the market began to come alive. Interest rates dropped from 12 to 9%. The market responded. In the next 5 years my income more than doubled, and then tripled! The brutal grind had evolved into a healthy market. Professional and economic success had finally arrived. Persistence and stubborn determination had begun to pay off.

Fast forward forty years.

I've survived four economic slumps and one major economic crash. My client base now numbers well into the hundreds. My sales are well into the many millions of dollars. My practice is rock solid. I found a way to survive and thrive. I can now settle into semi-retirement comfortably. And it only took 40+ years.

But what about you? How will you do? Most of us are familiar with the statistics of small business. Well over 80% of ALL new businesses in the U.S. don't survive their first five years. Most realtors (somewhere around 90%[*]) walk away in 18 months.

That's the reason for this handbook.

The first goal of this handbook is to help you decide if residential real estate sales and marketing is for you. It is written to help you discover and appreciate your own personal talents and convictions. If you find out this business is for you, great, if not, then you haven't wasted much time and money.

The second goal of this handbook is written to assure your success. The wisdom I've gained (along with the experiences of hundreds of successful agents I've worked with through the years), has been assembled and organized within these pages.

Explore the possibilities. Could this become part of your new life? I hope so.

---

[*] National Association of Realtors statistics.

Introduction

Welcome to *Real Estate Rookie, The Handbook for Brand New Real Estate Agents.* It is intended to be clear, honest straight talk. Most of you have picked up this book because you are considering a career in residential real estate sales. I mention "considering" a career in real estate because you deserve to know right up front whether this job is one that will give you great satisfaction and a great living. Should you believe this is the life for you, the remainder of this book has been written to help assure your success.

How to Get the Most from This Book

I recommend you read the entire book through once. Let it sit for a day or so, and then re-read it cover to cover. Don't shortchange yourself. Perform the exercises suggested. Avoid cutting corners.

I will offer some business models you may wish to emulate, as well as some you may wish to avoid. When you are done reading, you will have a far greater understanding of this industry and the potential it holds for you.

Tips and Traps for you, the new agent, will be offered at the end of most chapters.

SECTION I

A Brief History of Residential Real Estate

NOT TOO LONG AGO, homes in the U.S. were bought and sold using a one-page contract. There were no lockboxes, no computers, and no cell phones. Local Multiple Listing Service (MLS) books showing all homes on the market were published bi-weekly. Agents had to pick up and return all keys from each brokerage in order to show buyers homes. Buyers were never expected to have a loan approval in place prior to purchase. Loans took months and months to be approved. Sellers stood by and waited. Home inspections did not exist.

When a home sale finally closed, the sellers often took a month to move out. No rent was asked for, and none was expected. Agents were responsible for the coordination and proper application of all closing statements and documents. Sellers and buyers attended closings at the office of the listing brokerage. Each family often sat across the table, smiling at each other and taking turns signing forms.

That was then, and this is now. Responding to the arrival of the Internet, today's world of real estate has emerged from the dark ages.

There are fabulous online photos and home listings. You can shop for homes all over the world with a simple click. It is instantaneous, and it is fun!

Purchase and sale contracts often exceed forty pages. Disclosures are highly detailed and change monthly. Inspection reports are chock-full of facts, photos, and opinions. They rarely come in at less than a hundred pages.

Showings and buyer feedback are set up electronically. All documents are delivered and signed electronically. When the deal finally proceeds to closure, buyers and sellers independently report to the office of their closing attorney, or they may sign remotely. Buyers and sellers no longer have the opportunity to meet. Agents rarely meet face to face or even converse on the phone. For the most part, texting has replaced email. People are busy. People are very busy.

Lots of change, isn't it? Massive, in fact. Your place is being saved for you here, but only if you appreciate your own strengths and weaknesses. As a new agent and entrepreneur, you will learn to become street-smart and savvy. This should increase your chances at success.

Why Most Agents Don't Make It

THE BARRIER TO ENTRY for the real estate business is low. Very low, in fact. Take some online classes or attend a real estate school in the traditional classroom setting. Don't misunderstand—the test is hard to pass the first time. You must study and focus. Don't take the test lightly. Sit for the national and state exams, and kaboom, you are a real estate agent. The process takes only a few months of intensive study.

The commitment of time and energy is initially high. Regardless, this license requires minimal training and virtually no experience. There are no degrees required, as in the fields of law or medicine. There is no journeyman or apprenticeship status that must be earned by working in the field for a number of years, as in the plumbing or electrical trade business.

The initial time commitment to enter the business is minimal. The initial energy that must be expended to gain a license is minimal. The initial expense of gaining a license is minimal. All of this translates into an "Everyone else is making all this money—I, too" mentality. Or this one: "I love to look at houses. I may as well get my license."

The essence of this chapter is this: Little to no career counseling is involved in obtaining a real estate license. Little to no formal pre-training commitment is required to obtain a license. Little to no education is required to sit for the exam. Little to no formal training exists in how to begin a new career in this business.

The inevitable result is that a staggering number of newly licensed agents in our country rarely survive past their second year in the business.

Year in and year out, the National Association of Realtors (NAR) reports that nine out of ten agents give up and wash out within eighteen months of getting their license. They give up. They fail. These statistics are real and have remained so for decades.

Just think—each year thousands of people waste all that time, all that money, and all that energy, only to walk away in a few months. Because it is so very easy to obtain a license, few new agents initiate the serious steps that must be taken to ensure their personal and professional success.

This is actually good news for you.

Success in any small business rarely happens overnight. And if you really know yourself well, work with your strengths and weaknesses, and maintain a stubborn commitment to becoming successful, you will likely rise to the top.

Why Only a Few Agents Succeed

So, what makes a great agent great? you may ask. Today, the job of an agent is to help families buy or sell homes with the least hassle and in the shortest amount of time. Obtaining the lowest purchase price for our buyers or delivering the very highest price for our sellers is our goal.

Each client arrives with differing temperaments, talents, and convictions. Each family is different. Every situation is unique. Each deal presents with a unique set of economic and emotional circumstances. Sometimes their priority may not be about the money. It may be more about time or the energy that the client must expend to buy or sell.

This is where you come in! As their agent, you will be trained to ask the right questions at the right time. You will listen intently to their answers and craft a plan and timeline to reach the goals of your client.

Truly successful agents tend to be blessed with certain natural personality traits. They are often people pleasers. They are servant leaders. They are great listeners, which allows them to uncover their clients' needs and deliver the desired result. They are empathetic. They are usually gifted with the patience of Job. They work well individually and in groups. They are organized, focused, and can be demanding of themselves and their clients.

Truly successful agents describe themselves as tenacious and stubborn. They possess a "never quit" attitude. Setbacks are merely motivators and educators for them.

A successful agent views any real estate transaction as solving a series of problems and issues, some known and many unknown. A true pro appreciates that avoiding or solving these issues is the real reason they have a job in the first place. Today's agent accepts the fact that each closing is their sole responsibility. Little to nothing happens until the agent nudges, guides, and shepherds each aspect of a closing. Any closed sale is the final product of the systems they have put in place and the patience, guidance, and skill of an agent and their team.

A great agent is like a great doctor, attorney, plumber, or electrician: they view themselves as troubleshooters. They are master problem solvers. "Whatever it takes" is their mantra. They expect the unexpected, never duck issues, and maintain total devotion to their clients.

A successful agent knows that when the sale is finally consummated, the client remembers, good or bad. The things they remember are each found in the actual process of the deal. Clients remember the time, energy, and money it took to grind through the process. They will never forget how well the process went for them. It's up to us to make sure they remember the process as trouble-free. This is hard work.

Other indicators of any successful agent include being coachable and trainable. They learn to use systems and checklists to manage each part of a real estate transaction. They learn to manage client expectations. They appreciate that losing clients or accepting criticism is another form of self-growth. They remain in education their entire career.

Does most of this sound like you?

I'll repeat my statement from above: any well-trained, fully committed, savvy, street-smart agent will thrive and grow in this business.

Some outsiders swear that artificial intelligence will take over our industry. Similar things were said about the creation of the MLS system way back in the mid-20th century. Those same people foretold our ultimate demise with the invention of the Internet. That's amusing.

My argument is that ain't gonna happen. Nope. Not true. Never will be true.

Why? Because human beings are extremely complicated creatures. Our daily life circumstances change constantly. Our intellect, our emotions, our wants, our needs, our strengths, and our weaknesses change by the minute. No computer, no artificial intelligence, and no other technology will ever keep up. Only a human can piece together the staggering personality complexities of another human. Add an entire family with their dogs, cats, parrots, and turtles—now all are part of the dynamics. Common sense indicates that our place as real estate agents in this chaotic environment will be assured for decades to come.

Here's what you should know and appreciate about your new venture:

You have decided to become an entrepreneur, a small-business person. You are about to become You, Inc.

Like any business, You, Inc. is responsible for everything. You find the clients, you buy or sell their properties, you solve the problems, you close the deal, you pay the overhead, you pay the expenses, you, hopefully, make a profit.

There will be no base salary. There will be no company-paid insurance. There will be no company-paid 401(k). There is no punching the clock—no set time to come in, no set lunch times, and no set leaving time. You determine the hours you work and days (or weeks or months) you take off. You devise your own business plan. At first, you are likely to be the only person to hold yourself accountable for hourly, daily, and weekly tasks. Your future is now in your own hands. Welcome to residential real estate.

The Present and Future
of the Real Estate Business

CONSUMER CONFUSION IS AT AN ALL-TIME HIGH. The residential real estate business is morphing, changing, and evolving by the minute. Huge corporations like Zillow, Trulia, and Open Door have entered the business to compete directly with you, the agent. They are backed by billions in capital. They offer highly sophisticated software models to attract consumers. Really?

Instantaneous investors appear from all over the world, begging to buy residential homes. Right.

Airbnb and similar businesses offer homeowners opportunities for an income stream that never existed before. They forget to tell you how hard you will work for your money.

Supposedly sophisticated algorithmic calculations provide buyers and sellers with critical information on specific home values. I respectfully disagree. Only a well-trained agent who actively practices in a specific neighborhood can tour a home and apply the skills needed to evaluate a given property.

Our industry has now attracted classically trained new agents and people who see this as a true business. By that I mean newly licensed agents with MBAs and fully fleshed out business plans will likely be in the office next door to yours. They may be single agents or teams of agents, but they are here competing against you and intend to take no prisoners. They have done their homework upfront.

Some of today's new and improved agents are not agents at all, but teams of agents. The duties that a single agent once performed are now divided into many varied areas of responsibility. Teams now include a buyer's specialist, showing specialist, administrative business manager, lead-generation specialist, listing specialist, closing specialist, or customer-relations specialist. These teams are here to stay and are gaining their share of the business. We will talk more about this model in later chapters.

WARNING: *When you choose any new professional field, you must become totally dedicated to making it work.*

TRAP: *Half-baked commitments will doom you.*

Think for a Second About What Makes You Special

Nᴏɴᴇ ᴏꜰ ʏᴏᴜʀ ᴄᴏᴍᴘᴇᴛɪᴛᴏʀs can practice real estate the way that you will. None.

Your unique personality, together with your focus and your drive, will soon compete effectively with all the others. The care and commitment you show each client will not be matched by any of your competition.

No one can be you, ever.

So, let us think about what is going to make you stand out, what is going to make you unforgettable to your clients. What makes you unique or special? Where might you fit into this industry? The following ten challenging questions have been curated specifically to help you get a firm grip on whether to join this highly competitive industry.

Take your time; be deadly serious when you answer each of these. Your future depends on it.

QUESTION #1: *What is the "grand purpose" of your life?*

Define the mission of your business and what part it will play in your grand purpose in life. Define your vision for your business. What's it going to look like? How will your clients describe you and your business? What will they say about you as a person? Why will they say it? How does all of this align with your personal values and beliefs?

Think about it this way: At the end of your career, what do you want your business and your life to look like? What will your family's life have been like? Who will you have served? How well will you have performed? What will you have attained?

Why is it you really want to get into the residential real estate business? Is it for the money?

Nothing wrong with that. Not at all. Consider these national stats: The average Realtor™ earns $41,800 a year (circa 2017, NAR stats). That's before the expenses are taken out. You know, your car, gas, insurance, realtor fees, signs, lockboxes, desk fees, websites, business cards, marketing and advertising, etc. Hmm . . .

It's not all bad news, however. Ten percent of agents make more than $110,000 a year (circa 2017, NAR Stats). Yep, you haven't taken out your operational expenses yet. Let's do the math. Many agents have expenses (including company split) that run 50-60 percent of commissions. Can you support yourself and your family on the remainder? This is pretty important stuff here, isn't it?

So, like almost all sales jobs, in all industries, a tiny percentage of the salespeople actually win a disproportionate percentage of the total business. This phenomenon is so pervasive, it has its own name: the Pareto Principle, or the 80/20 rule. Some say that 20 percent of the agents sell 80 percent of the real estate. In some years, 10 percent of the agents sell 90 percent of the real estate. Here's a little surprise for you: only 1 percent will make serious money, potentially hundreds of thousands of dollars.

Is part of your grand purpose about gaining and maintaining your independence? Perhaps it's not all about the money for you but more about the freedom! We just mentioned all the freedoms involved in being your own boss. You can choose to sleep in some mornings, go to all the kids' games, help out at the school or church, take long weekends . . . Ah, the life. But is this accurate?

Nope. Not at all. Not at first, anyway.

When you first begin any business, in any industry, your life will seem to spiral and gyrate out of control. "Freedom" for you will be delivered in tiny bits of time between classes, hiring and interviewing, buying software, attending public and private events, or simply focusing on accomplishing everything in your business plan.

Okay. I may have misspoken about being your own boss. When you finally pick up some clients, you will quickly realize that you have now gone from being your own boss to reporting to more than just yourself. For each client you bring on, you have added an additional "boss." Your clients have engaged you to advocate for them and them alone. Your clients don't care that you may have ten or fifteen other clients. After all, to them, it IS all about them. That's why they hired you. Realize and appreciate that, as you grow your client base, your duties and responsibilities will grow.

The truth of your grand purpose should now be clearer, more self-evident. You are about to start your own business, and the success of your venture is going to challenge you and your family. The ultimate success in reaching your grand purpose must become the driving force behind entering the field of real estate. Failure for you is not a choice.

QUESTION #2: *Socrates once expounded, "To know thyself is the beginning of wisdom."*

This next exercise will be fun. After all, it is ALL about you! This is the part of this book where you figure out the traits of your personality. You are about to discover what makes you *you*.

Below, you will find a list of personality profiles. Check each of them out.

123test.com
16personalities.com
humanmetrics.com
gallupstrengthscenter.com

Take the time to perform at least two of these profiles. Perhaps the entire group. After all, you are preparing to go out on your own. I think you're worth it, don't you?

Go ahead and do this now. Your success depends on it.

Okay, you have likely seen some things about yourself that you've realized all your life. You may also have discovered some strengths you may have missed. You may want to talk with your family, friends, and those who love you about your results. See if they agree with the profiles.

You may find that the profiles indicate that your success lies in working in areas other than real estate sales. This is a good thing. You now know more than you did before! If real estate remains a strong area of interest, keep on reading. Simply realize that you may find you're more suited to administrative work, managing and running an office, loan underwriting, or even appraisal. There are lots of ways to use your skills in the real estate world.

Let's say you've studied your profiles. You have made your decision. Residential sales is the path you want to take. Good. In the pages to come, we will look at several different specialties that most suit your personality.

QUESTION #3: *How do your personality traits determine the likelihood for success in direct residential sales and marketing? I'm a member of a Facebook group of agents, LabCoat Agents. When I asked the group why they believed they survived past the two-year mark, here is what they said:*

"People said I would fail. It only made me more determined to succeed."

"'Don't quit your day job,' they teased . . . This made me even more determined."

"True grit and white-hot drive."

"I had no other choice. I had to succeed; there was no other way out."

"Whatever it took—if it was legal, I did it."

"I was desperate, actually."

"Lots of support from my family, emotional and monetary."

"I made a plan, I dove into education, and I followed through on my promises to myself, my family, and my clients."

You probably agree that these statements are true about any successful entrepreneur from any industry. It takes a special person to succeed as an entrepreneur.

This is what is so fun about starting your own business! When you know yourself, realize what you want out of life, and have the determination to succeed, you will find a way. Your stubborn determination, along with excellent training, perseverance, and TOTAL focus on your clients' BEST interests will set you up for success.

QUESTION #4: *What sort of practice do you want your shop to become known for?*

What will your reputation be in your market? Will your clients become loyal and devoted to you? What will they say to others about you? When the conversation turns to home buying and selling, will they think of you first? Will they jump at the chance to brag about you and refer you?

So, if you feel you have the temperament and desire to care for and love your clients, and to demonstrate the patience and skill it takes to maneuver complicated contracts and deadlines, this job may be for you.

QUESTION #5: *Do you actually enjoy helping people?*

Do you enjoy learning all about their joys, their fears, their goals? Do you get all fired up to discover what it is a family really wants and figuring out how to help them get it? Do you anticipate challenges and problems that must be overcome? How good are you at managing other people's expectations? How good are you at conflict resolution? Do you see yourself as a troubleshooter? I sure hope so.

QUESTION #6: *How well do you handle rejection?*

Most of what you will do each day will fail to produce a sale. "No, not today." "The deal fell through." "I lost my job. I can't buy the home now." "Why are you calling me?" "I hate you! All you want is my money!" "Go away!" "We decided to go in another direction; we've hired another agent."

Same ole, same ole. The true winners know that rejection will pave the way to profits. We all know that learning and wisdom are the products of rejection and mistakes made.

Our most successful agents simply shrug their shoulders and say, "Rejection is a major part of this business—you get used to it." "The more noes I get, the closer I am to a yes!" "I just got fired; I'll learn from it." "I'll move on!" "Next!!"

QUESTION #7: *How's your economic situation?*

Include in your first year's budget the start-up costs to begin your career: schooling, signs, website, business cards, local MLS dues, errors and omissions, housing. Not to worry. Your managing broker will help you with this.

Just in case you start off slowly, you may want to bank six months to a year of living expenses. This should alleviate some of the pressure. Appreciate and respect this, because from contract to close on any deal may take months or even up to a year. Prepare yourself and your family for this. If you follow this handbook, and focus on your clients' best outcome, you will soon have a pipeline of closings each and every month. You will likely make more money and have more fun than you may have experienced in your previous profession.

QUESTION #8: *How's your health?*

What's up with your mental and physical state? The early years in this business are the toughest. Pay attention to your mental and physical stamina. Schedule gym time. Build in time for your friends and family. Continued education will enhance your practice and bolster your confidence. Buy-in from your immediate family will directly impact your energy levels.

Successful agents I spoke with make appointments to work out, do yoga, or go to fitness classes, such as Pilates. They make formal appointments with mentors, coaches, and advisors. They realize that the ongoing maintenance of good mental and physical health is key to business success. They know that confidence, stamina, and courage improve as focus on health grows.

QUESTION #9: *Who's in this with you?*

I know I just mentioned this, but it deserves its own question. What does your family think about this new journey? The support of your family and friends will become a huge asset and source of comfort, especially at first. They need to realize and appreciate the fact that you are starting a new business. The hours will be long, the days and weeks longer sometimes. A life out of balance will become the norm. Make sure they see, appreciate, and support the payoff.

Family and sometimes friends will likely pick up the slack while you are off becoming wonderful and delivering a better life for your clients.

QUESTION #10: *Are you a goal setter?*

A new book is written each year outlining the virtues of goal setting. That is because goal setting works. The goals you set for yourself and your business may be simple at first, or they may be grandiose and massive.

Never mind the size and scope of your goals. Set some. All successful agents set goals. They don't just set *sales* goals. They set goals for their health, emotional goals, spiritual goals, and family goals. They write them down. They set a schedule for attaining them. Most goals are written to represent a year, three years, five years, and beyond.

Setting goals sparks organization and sets expectations. Goals beget certain standards that you feel must be met. Standards serve as a set of guidelines and protocols. Standards energize you, your team, and your family.

Accountability comes next. Formal accountability is defined as the structured and daily attention to the accomplishment of your goals. No one will do this for you, nor should they. Some agents find an accountability partner. They meet face to face or via phone at least once a week. You may choose to set parameters, establish rituals, and have timelines. All depends on you and your personality. There's no right or wrong. The bottom line is simply that you attain the goals you set for yourself. It may be as simple as this: Write a list of your goals on an index card. Carry it in your pocket. Read it out loud each and every morning. Yep, it is as basic as that. Try it. It works. I promise.

TIP: *Take your time answering these ten questions. Be honest with yourself.*

TRAP: *Should you choose to take these questions lightly, the results may disappoint you.*

SECTION 2

Preparation for the Test

DEPENDING ON THE STATE in which you practice, you will be required to attend classes, online or in a classroom setting. You must sit for and pass a real estate exam.

Some candidates prefer online classes. The advantage here is that you set your own schedule and learn at your own pace. Others enjoy the classroom setting. The advantage of this type of training is that you capitalize on the chance to learn from others.

Many classroom teachers actively practice real estate. Some simply teach. Those who actively practice will add tremendous insight into the business. Another potential advantage of the classroom experience is that you will meet other aspiring agents just like yourself. As time goes by, you will likely run into them again. Who knows? You may do lots of deals with them or even become partners one day. I suggest going to brick-and-mortar classes if at all convenient.

Should you want to be thorough and fully prepared, visit the sites I've listed below. They will help you prepare for your test:

thenightbeforetheexam.com

prepagent.com

compucram.com

YouTube offers a myriad of real estate test preparation tutorials.

Different Strokes for Different Folks

You have now answered the ten basic questions from Chapter 5. You realize that your own temperament, your own natural and developed talents, and the level of your conviction will determine your future in this business.

I'd like to introduce you now to two people who became agents at about the same time. They were from the same town, yet had never met. Though fictional, they are the product of "true to life agents" I have known over the past forty years of practice.

Their personalities were different. Their motivations for entering the business were different. Their grand purpose was different. Let's call them Joe and Marie.

Joe and Marie were in the same place you are now. They were brand new to real estate.

They were fresh out of real estate school, wet behind the ears, and ready to finally join the ranks of entrepreneurship and small business.

Meet Joe first.

Joe was a hard-charging corporate national sales manager of a local, family-owned manufacturing company. He had grown up in this town, the star quarterback of his high school; he'd played small-college football, where he took his team to the league championship. All the girls called him "ruggedly handsome." He had always viewed himself as a winner. He doted on competition. He loved to win, regardless of the cost.

Joe had joined his employer right out of college, a small, family-owned company that sold its products nationally. Joe was talented and over time, moved from sales associate to sales manager to director of national sales. He was proud of the fact that he had pulled himself up by his bootstraps. He'd worked hard and remained loyal for many years.

As director of sales, Joe was also proud of the fact that he had helped grow the company from a small organization to a major force in their industry. He felt it was his sales division that had made the company so successful.

Joe knew how to get things done! He was aggressive and focused on growing the company's sales and his own reputation. He just knew that one day the family would sell out to him or at least offer to let him buy into the company. Why wouldn't they? They needed him. He and his talented group of sales wonders were critical to the future of the company. It was only a matter of time now. He was sure of it.

Only one small problem nagged the family. They never seemed to be able to warm up to Joe as a person. They paid him very well. His salary and bonus were substantial enough to keep him around. They loved his drive and abilities but secretly never felt comfortable enough to offer him equity in their company.

Then, one day it happened. Out of the blue, the family sold out. They sold to a huge hedge fund.

Joe was devastated. He believed that the family would have come to him first—to seek his wise counsel, to appreciate all the things he had done for the company. Needless to say, Joe was disillusioned, frustrated, and hurt.

The new buyers were part of a massive conglomerate of similar industries. The handwriting was on the wall. His time was going to be very limited. He began to plan his escape. This time he would fully control his own destiny. He was going to find a business he owned by himself. His hunt began in earnest.

Over the years, Joe had become a more than casual observer of the local real estate market. He'd watched as some counterparts entered residential real estate and did well. It was clear to Joe that these guys were not nearly as talented as he was. Joe realized his skills were fully transferable. His skill set would likely translate into a career that he was fully in charge of. Time to make that leap of faith. Time to get into the world of residential sales.

This would be a breeze for him. His 401(k) was in good shape. He and his wife had made good money and invested wisely. Soon, Joe gave his notice, packed up all his trophies and sales awards, and never looked back.

Joe brought his office manager with him. Her name was Joanie. They were a team. Joe was helpless without her. She was used to Joe and his personality. She knew his strengths and weaknesses. She patiently organized Joe's business and kept him on track. She ran his back office brilliantly. Joe was the big-picture guy. Joanie ran the show. Perfect.

Joe had been married to his wife, Linda, for thirty years. They'd met in college. She had been a cheerleader for the small college he'd played for. She had been an excellent mom and patient wife. She'd raised their three children, mostly while Joe worked out of town.

One of their kids was now out of school and had moved to another state. The remaining two were still in university. Linda was a stay-at-home mom. She doted on her girls and her husband. Her house was clean, tidy, and buttoned up. Their family was used to Joe never being home. He made it in for the weekends, and many of those Saturdays were spent at the club, playing golf. Joe's family had its usual challenges, but overall, they were your all-American family.

Joe and Joanie went straight to online real estate school. They prepped for the exam and passed it on their first try. Life was chaotic and hectic at first. The culture shock included not only learning an entire new industry but also designing and maintaining a whole new business plan. Joe had sales and marketing down to a fine science. His introduction to all the remaining aspects of a small business was mind-boggling. Setting up his own LLC, buying all his own business equipment, choosing all the insurance plans and accounting systems. The process took time, which drove Joe crazy. He needed to sell something! In a few months, they had their act together. He had gone to all the training and taken all the new agent courses. Joe began to sell homes.

And now, I want to introduce you to Marie.

Marie had spent her life as a middle-school teacher. She was petite, hardly five feet tall. Her strawberry-blond hair, quick smile, and searing blue eyes drew plenty of attention when she walked into a room. She'd earned her undergraduate degree and master's in education from a private school out East. Her gifts were that she read people well, listened to her students, and was a master of motivation.

Marie had taught seventh- and eighth-grade English for the past twenty years. It so happened that she'd taught all twenty years at the same school, where she had a reputation for being demanding and tough. She also had a reputation for being kind, thoughtful, and caring. The old saying at the school was, "You prepare for Marie because she demands it." Also, "If you stumble, she's there to kick your butt and then hug you." She was an exceptional and rare talent. She'd taken home the Teacher of the Year awards consistently. Needless to say, she became an icon in her field.

Her two children were each preparing to enter college, one as a freshman, the other to law school. Her husband was an in-house corporate attorney, and together they made a good living. They were also prudent and conservative in their spending. Savings were long ago in place for the kids' college accounts. Both children wanted post-graduate degrees. They soon realized this was not going to be enough to maintain their lifestyle.

Twenty years in the education business had matured Marie. She had loved guiding and motivating young lives, but it was time to move on. Rising inside the school system entailed the field of administration, which brought its own set of pain and headaches. The salary boost was minimal. This was not what she wanted to do.

Marie had some close friends in the real estate business. They had independently encouraged her to consider joining them in buying and selling homes for clients. She realized the market was healthy and the town was growing. Interest rates were low and rates steady. Hmm . . .

She discussed her plans with her family. Together they mulled over the fact that her set salary and benefits would soon disappear. Finally, she made up her mind. Spring classes brought the close of school.

Her going-away party was warm, wonderful, and tear-filled. She cleared out her desk, put it all in one box, and headed for home. All her awards and certificates did not have to make the trip to her new office. They were packed away somewhere in the garage. It wasn't about the notoriety for her. It was about the future of her kids. Summer was here, and so was real estate school. Online classes were offered, but Marie valued the things the classroom experience would offer. The collaboration and group learning of a classroom environment were what she knew.

She was well prepared for each class. Her instructors were real-life successful agents and shared secrets not found online. She studied hard and asked lots of questions. Discussions would sometimes spark lively debate and extend after classes. She loved it. She was all over this learning thing. Boom! The tests came and went for Marie. She passed with flying colors.

Joe and Marie were switching careers at mid-life. It just so happened that they came into real estate at the same life stage. They were mature and had learned some key lessons. They wisely chose to approach their business based on how they perceived their own weaknesses and strengths. As this book progresses, you will discover how each of them chose to grow their practice and live their own best life.

Keep in mind that, although they are not real people, their journeys are. They are made up of people I have spent many years working with, conducted many deals with, and grown to love and respect—or avoid—working with.

TIP: *Most successful agents are dedicated to the achievement of their own grand purpose. As this book continues, you will discover more about your own.*

TRAP: *Keep an open mind at all times as you move through this book. There are secrets within its pages that may pertain only to you.*

Capitalize on Your Unique Skill Set

For you, just for you, I ask now that you return to the results of your personality profiles. You've likely discovered some aspects of yourself that will dovetail nicely into our field. Let me ask you some more questions. What fires you up about residential real estate? Where is it that you may excel and grow? There may be an area of focus for you that will bring you joy. Let's find out now.

Below is a series of specific areas of residential real estate. Move slowly through each group as they are described to you. Where do you see yourself fitting in? What is it about certain roles that attracts you the most? What is it about others that turn you off? How does the income potential meet your needs and goals?

For this book's purposes, we are going to focus on just residential real estate, not commercial.

Sales and listings of single-family homes
Sales and listings of luxury homes
Sales and listings of vacation homes
Sales and listings of condominium homes
New-home construction agent
Land sales
Residential property management and leasing
Sales and listings of foreclosures
Residential appraisal
Buyer's specialist
Listing specialist
Closing coordinator
Residential sales and listing assistant
Residential real estate teams
Developer/Builder
Investor
Flipper
Wholesaler

Here's a brief description of each profession:

Residential Listing and Sales

This model is the traditional agent practicing all types of real estate sales and listings. It includes all residential home types: single-family, condominiums, luxury homes, vacation homes, foreclosures, and land sales. You will be responsible for all aspects of any home purchase or sale. By law, you serve as an advocate for your clients' best interests and only their interests. You will initially work under the direct management of a licensed broker.

There are usually no salaried positions. Income is driven by the closings of sales. The more closings, the higher the income. Potential income is limitless. Most busy agents work forty to eighty hours a week. Sixty hours for an economically successful agent is an average schedule.

New-Home Construction Agent

Builders hire these agents to work full-time or part-time. This agent markets this builder's newly constructed homes. This type of agent may work independently or as a "captive agent" of a private single-home builder. They normally do not list any other homes for other builders, companies, or families. These agents represent the builder's best interests only. Depending on the nature of the market and the quality of the product, a properly trained new agent can earn well into the low six figures. There is usually no base salary. A seasoned, well-trained, savvy new-home construction agent may take home more than a mid-six-figure income. Most new-home agents work a minimum of forty hours a week, typically fifty to sixty. Weekends in the sales offices are pretty much required. Busy weekends can stretch well into the evening. New-home sales demand particular attention to details and exceptional organizational skills.

The upside of this business is that the expenses are nominal. National homebuilders offer excellent training. Smaller builders may lack this ability. The downside of the business is that, due to the local or national trends, the real estate market may deteriorate in only a few short months. Interest-rate volatility will also directly impact the market.

Residential Leasing and Management

This field traditionally offers several types of income potentials. The first is commission only; the second offers a minimum salary with commission or bonus.

In this position, you will be responsible to your principal to lease or manage their residential property, maximize rents, maintain tenant satisfaction, and minimize turnover. An exceptional leasing specialist knows how to close and loves it. Leasing specialists are naturally friendly, open to dialogue, and are people pleasers. Many leasing specialists evolve into the field of general real estate sales and listings. Income is often modest and into the mid-five figures. Hours of work are usually scheduled. Some weekend shifts will likely be required.

Property Management

Property managers are a different breed of agent. They may profile as introverts and are not usually sales-oriented. They work best in a formal and contained environment. They love working with numbers. Numbers tell the story for them. They manage and direct the proper application of systems and checklists. Their job is to focus on maximizing returns and minimizing turnover. They are highly detailed, rigid in attitude, and excel at working within specific rules and regulations. They work set hours for the most part, and their areas of responsibility don't change much from day to day. Income is in the form of a set salary and will occasionally include a bonus structure tied to raising income and mitigating expenses. Work hours are during the week and rarely on weekends. Expect salary to be in the mid-five figures to low six figures.

Sales and Listings of Foreclosures

Specializing in this field is sparked by local or national economic downturns. Most agents include this area of specialty into their normal work efforts when a market softens. Since the largest volume of repossessions normally takes place during downturns, most agents should not depend on this market to make a living. The work is highly specific and must be attuned to the lender involved. Highly skilled negotiators with a history of successful residential sales have made the most impact in this arena. Mature, savvy, and well-trained agents excel in this arena. Income is earned through commission only and is limitless.

Residential Appraisal

This field requires extended training and the attainment and maintenance of a specific license. Appraisers may be extroverted or introverted in personality and are great with details. Income range is wide—from $30k to $100k a year. Income growth is limited to the volume of work they can perform and their ability to maintain a quality end product. This field also demands particular attention to details and exceptional organization skills.

Buyer's Agent

This field requires a general real estate license. Buyer's brokers profile as energetic, friendly, open to dialogue, and are people pleasers. Most buyer's brokers are required by their brokerage to "lead generate" a specific amount of time each day. Their job is to locate, prequalify, and sign buyers to buyer representation agreements.

Buyer's agents must determine buyer needs, show potential homes, and help develop, write, and make offers on residential properties. They shepherd accepted contracts through all contract contingencies, negotiate exceptions and problems, and close sales. Buyer brokers may work independently or within a team. Certain teams will break out the responsibilities in a different manner than I just described. Work time can be managed and controlled.

Know this: income is by commission and totally dependent on the quality of training and the drive and desire of the agent to work overtime and weekends. A strong market, coupled with hard work, allows incomes to easily reach the low to mid-six figures.

Residential Listing Specialist

Most well-trained and confident agents will thrive in this arena. Their role entails meeting with homeowners, presenting a professional and well-prepared marketing plan, and successfully listing their home for sale. A skilled and successful listing agent must develop the skills to access each home seller's authentic desires and expectations. They gain homeowner trust and respect skillfully and with great confidence. They successfully acquire and maintain pricing strategies that maximize the final sale price of a home, yet minimize the time a home is on the market. Further, their job is to anticipate and solve the inevitable problems that accompany each sale.

The personality most suited for this job is a Type A personality. In the DISC personality profile, this person is a "high D." They are naturally aggressive, impatient, demanding of others, and, with proper training, an excellent closer. Their EQ (Emotional Quotient) is often off the charts. They possess the natural ability to read people, ask the right questions, answer each concern honestly and upfront, and respond to each issue professionally and on time. Managing each workday with skill directly affects income. The more listings and closings, the higher the income. The harder and longer you work, the more you make.

This specialty generally offers the highest income potential. Strong markets and excellent training will deliver high-six-figure incomes.

Closing Coordinator

Agents who choose this field are extremely well-organized and focused. They are hired by an agent or agent team and are paid to manage a home sale from the signing of a contract to the final closing. Most closing coordinators are licensed agents and work directly for independent producing agents on a per-closing basis. Many agents actually set up a business providing closing services and nothing else. Maintaining closing volume and attention to detail are the success factors in this field. Income varies but can easily attain the low-six-figure range when working with high-volume listing agents. Some superstar CCs work for an entire firm of agents.

Residential Sales and Listing Assistant

This person offers a similar set of abilities to that of a closing coordinator. Detailed-oriented and very well-organized, they basically run the business for a top-producing agent or firm. They usually have their license and can often take over some of the responsibilities of marketing, software management, database management, personnel management, and training for remaining staff. For all intents and purposes, they serve as the COO of a single practicing realtor and their team. A seasoned and skillful sales and listing assistant can make into the mid-five figures. Some assistants who work for high-producing agents can enter the six-figure arena.

Residential Real Estate Teams

This is a relatively new business model that involves dividing the various aspects of a regular agent's duties into specific and defined job functions. Many teams have a lead agent who owns their brand. For instance, some agents market their own brand (their company name) to the general public. The team may work under the umbrella of a separate managing broker (Coldwell Banker, Keller Williams, etc.), while their brand points the general public directly to their brand name. One example is the Anderson Group, powered by Keller Williams.

What a team actually offers is a group of very well-trained people who have been hired to list, sell, and buy properties for their clients. These specific jobs may include listing specialists, database managers, administrative assistants, buyer's agents, lead-generation specialists, and marketing specialists. The advantage of this type of model is that each area of specialty requires limited training and limited responsibilities. The advantage for newly licensed agents is that they can become productive far more quickly, limit their responsibilities, and maintain their quality of life. Commissions will be split among all the team members. This requires a team owner/agent to be highly skilled in evaluating, managing, and motivating true talent. They are usually veterans of the real estate wars long before they expand into their own team.

The downside for a single agent is that the commissions are shared with the entire group. A single agent moves along only at the speed of the group. Should you join an exceptional team, your income can reach well into the six figures. The owner/broker of a team can net seven figures.

Like any small business, owning and managing your own team can be a blessing or a curse. A team owner's responsibilities are greatly expanded from that of a single agent. Income is virtually limitless, and success is fully dependent on how well the agent/broker can locate exceptional talent and evaluate, hire, train, and manage each group member.

Developers, Builders, and Agents

Most agents who build or develop housing are usually more mature in the industry. They have formed strong contacts and past work history within the local governments, construction groups, and lenders. Development and building—by its very nature—is a high stakes, high-risk business. Local real estate markets as well as money markets can change long before a developer's product hits the market. Potential income may go from losing it all to making many millions in a few short years. High risk, high reward.

Real Estate Investor

This field is an exciting avenue for any agent to explore, especially after they gain some traction and learn more about the residential industry. Many agents learn the basics of real estate investment early in their career and make it a focus of their wealth-building as time goes on. Successful real estate investors have learned how to buy low and sell high. This takes years of experience. Experience is defined as making lots of mistakes and learning from each of them.

Investment real estate can begin with small initial investments by locating and buying duplexes, triplexes, and multi-unit rentals.

Economic risk drops dramatically as the newbie investor applies the proper level of education and skills. Time devoted to managing investments will vary by investment. Moderate to extreme risk is involved. Potential income and losses for investors will range from massive failure to unlimited profits.

Old timers say real estate investing is simple, but not easy.

I've been blessed through the years to meet and work with many investors, some with virtually no formal education, who became multi-millionaires many times over. They started out small, worked their tails off, made many friends, paid their debts, took their licks, and never gave up. They bought their real estate with the sole purpose of holding over a long period of time. They rarely sold anything. Quietly, they assembled massive portfolios with no debt, consistent cash flows, and staggering profits. Income here can be unlimited.

Flippers

Flippers may be agents or investors, or a hybrid of both. They locate, finance, buy, renovate, market, and resell homes, duplexes, triplexes, apartments, or even commercial buildings. Successful flippers are usually seasoned, well-trained, and sophisticated risk-takers. They have developed relationships with lenders/banks and the various trades (roofers, plumbers, electricians, etc.) They buy low and sell high. Flipping takes place most profitably during economic downturns. The reasons for this are myriad, but suffice it to say many people are running away from real estate when these guys are buying. Savvy buying and selling is the key to success. Risk can go from minor to massive. Successful flippers exhibit street smarts and an "uncommon level" of common sense. Income for flippers will range from major losses to unlimited returns. Some flippers don't flip. They buy, renovate, lease, manage, and hold. Income can be unlimited.

Wholesaler

A wholesaler is an investor who locates residential buildings and negotiates, buys, and takes ownership of properties. Their goal is to improve property value through rezoning, rehabbing, removing, rebuilding, or simply outright selling them without change at all. The difference between the price they pay and price they ultimately sell for is the basis of this business model. Wholesalers buy low and sell high. They may perform as real estate agents, non-real estate agents, or investors. These professionals get more and more sophisticated in their art through trial and error. Similar to developers, builders, investors, and flippers, a wholesaler's income will range from huge losses to unlimited gains. Risk is reduced by excellent training or partnering with seasoned professionals. Income can be unlimited.

TIP: *More than a few of these professions may appeal to you at first. When you are new, take the time to learn the basics. Real Estate 101 must come first.*

TRAP: *Shortcutting the learning of the basics in any industry is unwise.*

Joining the Best Company (for You)

THERE IS NO RIGHT WAY OR WRONG WAY HERE. Plan to take your time. Arrive at each interview very prepared. Research each firm well before you get there. Ask lots of questions.

Locate and choose at least three companies with good reputations in your market. Then call to set an interview. Try to schedule it on a busy day, when the majority of their agents will be in the office. Ask to attend their weekly, biweekly, or monthly staff meeting. Go in, sit down, watch, and listen. Your gut will tell you a lot. Do you know some of the agents of this company? What are they like? Why are they successful? Why are they working with that particular company?

Your initial interview will likely be with the company owners/executives or recruiting specialists. Accept the fact that they have held hundreds of these interviews. It's a primary objective of theirs to grow the company. Observe their overall attitude and demeanor toward you. What sort of vibe do you pick up from them, their staff, or even the people in the hallway? Is the office clean and updated? Does there seem to be a "hum" of energy about the place?

Let's expand on your interview for a minute. Do the people you are speaking with seem interested in the money you bring to them or in helping develop your career into a long-lasting business? Ask about the company's mission, vision, and values. Sounds hokey, I know, but this is important to know. What is their grand purpose? What's it all about for them? Their answers will be very telling for you.

How many agents do they have? What is their turnover rate? Do their agents practice in the traditional manner, or are they specialists in a specific field? Do they introduce you around the office? Do they take you on a quick tour?

What kind of training do they have? Is there a fast-track program to gain income and traction quickly?

How does this company use technology to locate buyers and sellers? Is there a formal mentoring program?

How will you be paid? How are the splits set? In other words, out of each closing, what does the firm collect from your sales, and what do you receive? Is there a cap on what you pay the firm each year from your commissions? Once you hit a certain level of production, do you keep more of your commissions? Do you ever get to keep 100 percent of your commissions?

Is there profit sharing in this company? How does it work? Some companies offer stock. How do you participate? What is the track record of the stock? Are there dividends paid in the good years? How liquid is the stock? Can it be sold or traded?

Initiate Guerrilla Tactics

Dig a bit more. Attend open houses hosted by the agents of the companies you're considering. Walk right in the front door. Introduce yourself. How do they respond to you? Do they exhibit professional-ism, training, and skill? How do they handle the guests who walk in? You will learn a lot. I promise.

Here is a technique some agents have used effectively in the past: Ask whether the firm you're considering maintains offices outside your market area. If they do, go online and locate a few offices. Pick one or two agents in those offices to call. When they answer, describe where you're from and explain to them that you are choosing a company to work with and that their company (located in your town), happens to be one of them. Ask permission to ask questions. These guys have no dog in the fight. They will likely be upfront and honest with you.

Following your interviews and based on the information you assemble, you will likely make your first big business decision: choos-ing a company to affiliate with. Good for you. Do it.

Remember, it's not over till it's over. Do-overs are welcome! You are an independent contractor! As an independent contractor, you can take your license with you at any time. Be bold when you find that your pres-ent firm is not helping you grow and thrive. Take what you've learned from this experience. Move on to a company that supports your vision.

I now return to our mythical new agents, Joe and Marie. Let's take a look at how each of them chose their first company.

Joe was in a terrific hurry. He felt that he had developed a legend-ary past career in national sales. He and his group had far exceeded their sales goals each year. He enjoyed a national reputation as one of the best in his field. He was proud of his record.

When it came to choosing a real estate company, he considered only one the leading luxury company in their town. This group was small and family-owned. They offered few in-house training programs. This firm had looked to their local board of realtors to handle most of their education needs.

Joe knew some of the agents of this firm from his golf club. This little company would surely turn out to be a good match for his talents and expectations. He fully intended to sell nothing but luxury homes, so this was the agency for him. He would conquer this business just like he had his old one.

Joe's new employer was well aware of Joe and his past successes. They went way out of their way to make him feel special and welcome. In fact, they offered Joe and Joanie their own private corner office, rent free. *Wow, this is more like it!* Joe thought to himself.

Marie took her time. She chose to interview at three companies, each of which had strong local reputations. She was systematic and thorough. All three companies offered compelling reasons for working with them. Marie visited open houses and paid attention to the hosting agents. She introduced herself to each agent and struck up easy, relaxed conversations. Within a few weeks, she finally chose the group that felt most comfortable to her.

TIP: *Interview with more than two firms. Things you may never have thought of will pop up.*

TRAP: *Know how deep the water is going to be before you just jump in. Does the firm you want to join dominate that part of the industry you want to specialize in? Is their training effective?*

By Now, You've Likely Chosen a Company to Hang Your License With

Your broker will likely offer a quick-start program similar to the wildly popular book written by Carla Cross, *Up and Running in Thirty Days.*

Take full advantage of the training. Get involved. Ask lots of questions. Soak it all in. A little secret: Discover how to help others first. Your positive, helpful attitude will help you feel welcome by your fellow agents.

As the weeks and months pass by, keep a watchful eye out for successful agents. You will hear about them or be introduced to them. They may, in fact, help teach classes to new agents in your company. Be sure to ask them how they became successful. Ask enough questions to discover what makes them tick, what makes them different. What sets them apart from the herd? How did they arrive, and how long did it take them? What mistakes did they make along the way? What makes them so special? How did they build a practice that has raving fans?

Remember to always show respect for the time top producers give you. They likely live by a preset formal schedule. Each day has been preplanned and written on a calendar. You can't expect to just walk into their office, plop down, and be welcomed with open arms. They will be short and brief and likely ask you to make an appointment. Don't take it personally; all the pros do this. That's just one of their secrets!

Oh, yeah—never forget that each agent, whether or not they're a top producer, is running their own business. They may not want to spend their time and energy to help you if they don't feel you're likely to become successful and reciprocate somehow. You must make it clear to everyone that you're determined to succeed and that you intend to help others do the same. You'll discover that, over time, you will find your tribe. You'll find those who align with your credo, your way of doing business.

Joe chose to blow off meeting any agents. He nodded, smiled, shook hands with each of them, made small talk, and moved on. His focus was laser-like. Total dominance of this industry was his goal. Meeting other agents seemed like a total waste of time. Joe viewed himself to be in direct competition with other agents. Besides, he believed himself to be far more talented. Friendships with other agents seemed to serve no purpose for Joe. He was totally focused on early personal success. He aspired to proving to everyone that he was, in fact, the new sheriff in town.

It was simple for Joe; he was to become THE number-one agent. His measuring stick was going to be total sales volume. Just like at his last workplace, Joe was the rainmaker. He was the man! He brought home the bacon. He relished his role.

His early months were spent learning the language of real estate. His mentors and coaches taught him that, when he asked buyers or sellers the proper questions, they would respond with the answers that he needed to motivate them. His trainers called this "scripts and dialogues." Each morning, he set aside an hour to practice his scripts.

Just like he did in his all-star years playing college football, he embraced and looked forward to honing his skills through practice. And just like in college ball, he would run the same play, the same scripts, over and over and over again, until each script became second nature to him. Just like in college ball, he would call specific plays for certain situations.

The drudgery was real. The practice hours seemed endless. Joe knew one thing: the grueling practice prepared him for the "big game." His toil and trouble paid off. Soon, he was winning the listings, pricing and positioning each home to be competitive in the marketplace.

Joe didn't stop there. He took every class his board offered. He traveled to other cities to gain more knowledge. Joe could not get enough training and coaching. His scripts evolved, and he became powerful. Just like with football, training was key. Joe's determination to succeed was raw and real. Joe decided that he was going to the top.

Marie approached her new career in a radically different manner. She chose a company that embraced collaboration. Her new position as part of a team was buyer's agent. Her responsibility was to find home buyers, isolate and focus on specific home choices, and close the sale.

Marie knew herself very well. She realized that, as a teacher, she had always been well-organized and focused. In the past, she'd worked from lesson plans that were designed to get results for her students. Twenty years of honing her teaching skills had taught her that a written plan for each day, week, and month relieved her stress and maintained her focus. This skill set was going to pay off for Marie.

As a buyer's agent, her team required that she learn the language of home buyers. She learned quickly that all home buyers face similar issues over and over again. Her team gave her the scripts and dialogues she was to use to discover what her clients really wanted in their new home. Each question was strategic in nature and designed to garner accurate and usable answers. Marie soon embraced her role. She awoke each morning with a sense of purpose and resolve.

Marie's team sensed her determination and interest. Her questions were well thought out and indicated her sincerity to learn. They welcomed her with open arms. They were keenly aware that her gentle, firm, and mature approach would be well-received by their clients. They felt they had found a rare and true talent, and they jumped at the chance to help her.

Let's talk about you for a minute.

Will starting your business as an independent agent, like Joe, work for you? Do you have the energy and drive to learn the scripts and dialogues it takes to gain new listings and attract home buyers?

Or would joining a team pay off for you? Here's how some teams are organized: One agent usually owns a team. That owner may name (or brand) the team after themselves. For example, "The Johnson Team" or "The Brandau Group" is a company set up inside a larger brokerage, as in "The Johnson Team," powered by Remax, or "The Brandau Group," powered by Keller Williams. Another may be simply the name (or brand) Two Doors, or YourAgent, or whatever.

Teams divide the responsibilities of a single agent into smaller, more definable responsibilities. Listing specialists, marketing specialists, buyer's specialists, business managers, lead generators, and closings specialists make up a team. Be sure to check them out with the brokerages you meet. The team concept may match your skill set.

If you choose to work with a team, your initial training will be focused on one specific specialty. The obvious advantage here is that you have far less to learn and that you will get up and running quickly. Your schedule will be more manageable. Your responsibilities will be limited. So will your income. You will be splitting a commission with many other people. Volume is the key, as well as increased accountability to your team. Many agents swear by this structure. Your dedication to the success of the team is paramount. The success of the team will be tied to your ability to perform your job and perform it very well. Your team expects and deserves results from each member. The satisfaction of reporting your weekly successes may be exciting and fulfilling for you.

There is no right way or wrong way to begin your career. Know yourself. Trust your gut.

Why did Marie choose to work with buyers right away?

Marie learned from her team leader that working with buyers early in her career offered several advantages. The first was that buying a home is not as stressful as listing and selling one. Home buyers are normally far more relaxed, positive, and excited than home sellers.

Sometimes, working with home sellers can be like herding cats. You must include each member of the family as a home seller. Each person living in the home will likely possess their own exclusive set of expectations. Mom, Dad, the kids, the dogs, everyone. It's your job to get everyone singing from the same page of music. It's also your job to keep the project in the middle of the road and moving on.

Home sellers sometimes place themselves under tremendous stress or set self-imposed deadlines that are unattainable. It takes skill and excellent training to serve these people and get to a win-win closing. You may be the type of person who welcomes these challenges.

Why did Joe choose to work with sellers?

Joe viewed listing and selling homes the way he viewed his old job at the plant.

Million-dollar sales at the plant were like million-dollar sales of homes. You just do it.

He was nervous at first, but his drive overcame his fear.

Obviously, Joe arrived as a brand-new agent with a tough skin and determined attitude. He meant business, and his sellers picked up on that. Joe exuded confidence. He was sometimes tough or abrasive. His body language and tenor often came across as impatient and hurried. This did not always work out well for Joe or his clients. On many occasions, it did.

All that training Joe absorbed introduced him to the very latest in Internet lead-generation systems. These systems were expensive, sophisticated, and effective. Joe's past skill set, along with the newly learned scripts and dialogues, taught him how to gain the trust of homeowners. He stumbled a bit at first. Soon he became a listing wild man. Joe was charming, well trained, short on small talk, and all business. Joe was rocking it.

The lightning-fast market drove most of Joe's home sales. He used the lack of supply to aid his sellers. He played hardball and usually attracted top dollar.

Depending on the nature of the market and the extent of your training, listing homes is far more beneficial to your long-term business than working strictly with buyers. Here's why: A properly trained agent will generate at least two home buyers from each listing. The home you have listed may not fit their needs, but something else will, and you are the person who finds it for them.

This, of course, will result in three closings: the first from the listing and the last two from the two new buyers you dug up or who impressed the seller down the street.

As a true pro, you will list a home for sale and saturate your neighborhood with their calls, door-to-door meetings, open houses, and direct mail. Your willful presence and your curious nature will leverage each single listing into multiple closings.

TIP: *Trust your gut. Get your feet under you with strong basic training.*

TRAP: *Keep your wits about you at first; if one avenue of this business doesn't seem attractive to you, you can always switch to another. It is not the end of the world.*

It's Time to Find
Some Clients

CONSIDER THIS CHAPTER your initial lead-generation strategy.

You now have your license, an area of focus, and a company to work with. It is now time to find some business. It's time to find clients to serve.

Rearranging the chairs on the *Titanic* did not work out well for anyone. "Getting ready to get ready" will not pay the bills. Setting up your desk with pictures of your kids and your dog will not find you clients. You can argue with yourself all day long that you don't know enough yet, that you are not prepared yet. Horsefeathers!

Every brain surgeon had to have a first patient. Any new attorney had to have a first client. Every journeyman plumber had to go out on their first service call by themselves.

Look at it this way: Your preliminary training is in place and complete. You are calling your immediate sphere of influence—those who know you, love you, and trust you.

You are probably going to stumble and bumble. We all screwed up early on. It's pretty much guaranteed that you will. It's like learning how to ride a bike. You will fall in the beginning, but once you get the hang of it, you will zoom.

Keep on keeping on. This is your time. Go find someone you can help buy or sell a home. Today. Now.

Here's how to relieve some stress when looking for clients: Your total focus must remain on your clients and serving their best interests. You will look out for them at all costs. You will ask the questions and formulate the strategies that prove to your clients that your interest is their interest. If you get stuck and don't have an answer to a question, go to your broker, coach, or to a more seasoned agent in your office. They will help; they remember being new, just like you. When your work reflects the fact that you are totally dedicated to your clients' best interests, your fear will evaporate. You will become energized in performing at a totally new level. Your clients will realize that you actually care about their well-being. They will relax and respond to you with respect and patience. I promise.

Remember, make your initial calls to those you know, love, trust, and respect. Call and ask them to join you for coffee. When you meet, tell them about your new business, why you chose this field, and why you love helping people find and buy homes. Ask them to consider referring you. Ask them for permission to follow up from time to time. Make sure you guarantee them that you will serve any referral they give you like your own family. Guarantee that you will not put pressure on any client and that you will follow up with the referring person in a timely manner and update them.

Promise yourself you will lead generate for two hours each business day and that you'll do so your whole career. Remember: no clients, no closings. Tip: Mornings from nine to eleven have proven to be the best times to catch people.

Joe had little fear. He had no jitters. He just needed to learn the language of real estate. Soon, and with some practice, he performed like the pro he knew he would become. Soon he realized that, in order to grow even more, he would need a coach or mentor.

Marie was a bit timid at first, but that went away quickly. She had done her homework and learned the scripts and dialogues required for a buyer's agent. She practiced with her fellow agents. She soon integrated her training into a systematic and very natural set of procedures.

Marie went right out and focused on refreshing old friendships and connections. She smiled when she talked on the phone. She was interested and authentic. She had a twinkle in her eye whenever she ran into former students and parents. They seemed to light up when she walked into any room. This was not as hard as she had first thought it would be. Marie was soon on her way.

TIP: *No one you call at first will expect you to be a superstar agent. They will welcome your call for a helping hand.*

TRAP: *Calling your sphere without the proper training will set your career back.*

Types of Lead Generation

THERE ARE AS MANY LEAD-GENERATION IDEAS as there are agents and personalities. Trust that the better any potential client knows you, or knows of you, the more likely they will welcome you as their agent. Some say that contacting your entire database thirty-three or thirty-eight times a year is the key to building and sustaining your business. Belly to belly, face to face will pay off for you.

Think about the real estate superstars you know now. They didn't start out as superstars. They likely clawed their way to the top, just like you will. They paid the price. They learned from their mistakes. They welcomed the daily grind. They never, ever gave up.

Here are a few ideas that have proven to work for agents:

1. Become well-known and respected in your communities and your tribes. This, of course, will take time. Remain dedicated and active from the start. Be visible and become noticed as a giver, not

a taker. Such groups may include your neighborhood association, your place of worship, your civic clubs, your athletic clubs, your country clubs, your PTA, etc.

2. OWN your farm. (See Chapter 21.) Proper training from your broker will set you up for success in initiating items 3–13 below.

3. Write lots of notes to your sphere of influence. Use any excuse to contact them: Birthdays, holidays, notes of concern, congratulations, etc. The point is to make contact and prove your interest in them.

4. Throw a kick-off party! Client-appreciation party! Christmas party! Winter-is-over party! Be clever.

5. Send video emails with monthly market updates to your database. Always give accurate and up-to-date information. Stay away from boring stats. Be animated. Exhibit energy! Smile! Prove to your group you are on top of the market.

6. Call your clients to check in with them. Calling just to say "Hello" shows you care.

7. Call FSBOs (For Sale by Owners), expired listings, and circle prospecting. Circle prospecting is knocking on all surrounding doors in a newly listed neighborhood and sharing your good news.

8. Work open houses for other agents. A well-trained agent and well-presented home will make you huge money.

9. Send out newsletters. Be different. Stand out. Prove you are smarter, quicker, and better than any other agent. Remember, when you are new, you can tell everyone that you'll bring far more time and energy to them than other, more senior-level agents.

10. Email your database monthly. Your brokerage will offer some insights.

11. Cold-calling. (Yep, it works.)

12. Door-knocking. (Yep, it works.) Secret: Always arrive with a small gift. Be energetic and interested in the homeowner. Take only a minute of their time, and then move on.

13. Pumpkin giveaways, meet-Santa extravaganza, Easter egg hunt. The list is endless. If there is a holiday or special day, make a big deal out of it.

14. Send out notes/emails/texts/emails offering TESTIMONIALS (from people who love you).

15. AFTER you've had some success (and made some money), check out some of these lead-generation companies. These are some companies that many successful agents use, with good results. Remember, this is real money you are spending, and it must be held accountable in order to produce triple what you are paying.

Boomtownroi.com

Brivity.com

SierraInteractive.com

Cincpro.com

Chime.com

Realgeeks.com

Zurples.com

Opcity.com

Gofindhome.com

Offers.com

Kunversion.com

Thesocialagent.com

Vulcan7.com

TIP: *This is a boatload of information to digest. Eat the elephant one bite at a time.*

TRAP: *Same as the last trap. Little to no professional training will set you back months and months.*

Chapter 13

Coaches, Mentors, and You

THIS IS ONE OF THE SINGLE MOST USED HACKS for new agents. Find yourself trusted coaches or mentors. They will accelerate your career. After all, their livelihood is dependent upon your success. The company you join may offer programs for mentoring or coaching. Some companies offer a managing broker or team leader as a mentor. This is excellent, especially at first, when your income is nonexistent. It is critical to your success that you take full advantage of this perk your company offers.

When you begin to make some spendable income, be willing to pay for more specialized, in-depth training. Ask around your agency. They will steer you to coaches who deliver!

Here's how I see the difference between a coach and a mentor. A coach makes their living from training alone. A mentor trains you for a minimal or no charge. Coaches normally do not practice real estate. Mentors, in this case, usually do.

When you hire your first coach, expect them to challenge you and hold you accountable for doing as they say. Any good coach will push you. Your early success and their income will depend on how well and how soon you produce. They will ask you to do things that are uncomfortable for you at first. Accept the challenges. Work through the pain. Change and growth is inherent to any new job.

Finding a good coach is a matter of checking with your network, researching online, and attending lots of trainings and events offered by your local board. Ask around, and interview several before hiring one. Be perfectly willing to fire any coach when they fail to triple your business. Yes, I said, "triple."

Joe had saved his money in preparation to begin his new career. He used some of it to interview and ultimately hire a coach who came to him as a proven commodity. His coach had sold millions in the past and coached many superstars. Joe wanted to be like his coach. Joe's coach assigned homework and demanded accountability. Joe and Joanie gained traction. They did exactly as their coach instructed, and soon their numbers began to soar.

Marie had joined a team as a buyer's broker. Marie did not hire a mentor or coach at first. Her training came from her team leader and classes offered through her company. She found that YouTube offered excellent educational videos hosted by real estate pros. She joined Facebook groups for buyer's agents. Her team was dedicated to her and supported her in this process. Slowly the lead-generation techniques she learned began to pay off. The hours and hours of hard work began to pay off in attracting clients and closing sales. Others heard about her care and concern for her clients. That alone began to pay off handsomely. She began to look forward to each morning and to another day of helping her clients. New clients seemed to come to her with positive expectations and trusted her without question.

So, do what Joe and Marie did. Take the classes, buy the books, and go to all the training you can, especially when you first begin. You are building the foundation for your success.

At first, Joe's sole attention was on responding to his coach's training. Joanie read Carla Cross's book and began to implement the strategies it offered. Joe was in a hurry. He was impatient and needed to make things happen quickly. Joe's coach explained to him that working with buyers took way too much time. Joe let others have that side of the business, for now. He went after home sellers.

Each morning, Joe embraced his new hotshot lead-generation companies and worked his leads. His scripts and dialogue training were paying off. In only a few months, he began to list and sell homes with more and more confidence.

As time went by, Joe found that he did not have much time to really get to know his clients. This was not the point for Joe. His dedication was to the closings and the sales he produced. Bonding was not his thing.

Just like at his old job, Joe produced volume—lots and lots of volume. Joe's sole focus was to get the job done and move on. This was purely a business for Joe. He saw little value in building relationships.

Joe worked day and night. His golf game and those friendships had to be set aside for now. His family sometimes took vacations without him. Joe was eating and sleeping real estate. He was honestly enjoying his business successes. He knew he could do it, and he was now proving it to everyone else.

Joanie, his Wonder Woman office manager, ran the back office in her usual masterful manner. Joanie was a savant with the details. She managed Joe and kept every detail of their business on track. Part of her job was to manage the Internet lead-generation systems and deliver a fresh set of potential clients each morning. It all seemed to be coming together rather nicely. Joe was blessed to have Joanie as a key factor in his business success.

Marie lucked out, too. She had joined a razor-sharp team, and she was about to improve on it. She didn't realize it when she arrived, but her team had been running for years before her arrival. All she had to do was learn the job, apply the principles of the training, and close delighted clients. She soon found that many of her past skills were transferrable.

As she did in the past, Marie produced a written plan for each day. She sat down every Sunday evening and outlined her upcoming week. Teaching had taught her to sit down for ten minutes every night and organize for the next day. She slept well because she felt she had a bit of control over her business. She was prepared. She was fully energized and ready to go each morning.

Marie learned quickly that the world of residential real estate can be wild and unpredictable. Each day arrived with new challenges and deadlines. No two days were ever the same. Her appreciation for excellent training was growing each month. Marie learned to take the time to explain her systems and checklists to her clients. It became obvious to them that her focus was always a successful outcome. She set boundaries and expectations for all groups involved in each closing: the other agent, the vendors, and the buyers. She taught them how she worked. They relaxed around her because they knew what to expect. They came to depend on her. Marie was building a rock-solid future for herself.

Marie also paid close attention to herself and her family. She set appointments that included working out and meditation. She scheduled at least one day off a week, a date night with her husband, or time with her close friends. She recorded every aspect of her life in her calendar. Marie and her family took two vacations a year. She realized that planning and arranging these adventures was almost as fun as the vacations themselves. This new business was starting out pretty well!

TIP: *Any business you enter brings its own grind. Welcome the grind. Keep a diary of each win and each mistake you make. Study your diary each day.*

TRAP: *You may get discouraged and bogged down from time to time. We all do. Return your focus to your grand purpose. Nothing will get in your way. Nothing.*

Your ONE Thing

Gary Keller, founder of Keller Williams, thought this point was so powerful that he and Jay Papasan wrote a book, *The ONE Thing*. It has become an international bestseller, and its secrets apply in all industries and walks of life.

Each evening, go to a quiet spot in your home. Sit down and write out your to-do list for the next day. Itemize the most important things on your checklist in order of importance. Get clear in your mind what must happen to attain your final goals.

When I first started out, preplanning the evening before a workday paid off for me. I'd transfer any undone items to the next day's list, again in order of importance. In the morning, I would begin by checking the status of each upcoming closing first. Closings meant income. Closings meant survival. That was the ONE THING for me in the beginning. Next up, I would check the status of each active listing and each buyer. Then came the lead generation. Over time, practicing this system resulted in a far more organized and focused approach to my business. I slept better each night. I woke up each day with a written plan.

We know now that total focus was not a problem for Joe. He maintained only one focus: sales volume!! Woohoo!! He was crushing it! Joanie took care of the nagging details.

Marie struggled at first, but work-life balance came for her by setting priorities on those things most important to her: family, health, mental energy, spirituality, and building a lasting client base. At first, her mornings were spent catching up with her past students and contacts. As time wore on, it was cold-calling and door-knocking.

TIP: *The ONE Thing is one of the best business/life books ever written.*

TRAP: *I spent the first thirty years of my career without its wisdom.*

The Most Powerful
Rookie Secret

Your first series of clients may be daunting for you. In fact, they may scare you to death. Good. From this point on, your total intention is to maintain complete focus on your clients. You should be laser-focused and dedicated to them and the successful outcome of their sale or purchase. That is all. Whatever it takes, however it must be done, you will be bright-eyed, full of energy, and fully attentive to your clients. You may be nervous. but your concern for them overrides your anxiety.

Right off the bat, your clients will notice your energy! They will appreciate your attitude and devotion. They will marvel that you listen to them and respond to their concerns. They will realize you are for real. They will be relieved. They will relax. They will open up to you. Soon, they respond to your questions freely and honestly. They have now become your clients and yours alone. You have arrived at your first success, well before any closing has taken place.

Joe knew no fear. He had won championships in the past, both on the football field and in industry. He knew it took devotion to training, proper diet, hard work, and intense focus.

Marie accepted fear as part of her new career. She knew she didn't know much at first and quickly admitted it when challenged. She also knew how to get the answers. Her focus at first was to prove to her clients how important they were to her. She knew how to make them feel special, just as she had her students.

Seven Houses

THIS IS THE NUMBER OF HOMES the average American will live in throughout their life. The number varies from time to time, based on the economy. Your goal is to help each and every family buy and sell ALL of them. That's seven home buys and seven home sales. Add it up. One client, one family, fourteen total sales. Let that sink in for a minute.

Your clients may even transfer out of state. Great! They will want YOU to find them an agent in the town they are moving to. They realize that one of the biggest profits (or losses) they may ever experience is in the purchase or sale of a home. They want you to find them a seasoned, reliable, and trustworthy professional. They want a new agent that is as good or better than you.

You may be a brand-new, raw rookie, but you bring one critical skill to the table: the fact that you CARE about your clients. You work hard to meet their goals. Their goals become your passion. They realize it. And they will never forget it. Boom. You are now successfully building your practice that will last a lifetime.

Take on the "seven houses" challenge. Promise yourself that you will strive to help each client buy and sell the homes they own through the years. It will pay off handsomely for you.

Marie always seemed to get the first call when her clients were thinking of moving or transferring. They depended on her and trusted her.

Joe counted on the Internet for his leads. His practice was fast and furious. There wasn't much time spent on building professional friendships. The market was too hot, and he was crushing it.

TIP: *Engender love and respect from your clients. Make it a goal of yours to keep each one for many homes to come.*

TRAP: *Counting on brand-new buyers and sellers year in and year out is a very expensive way to build a practice. Serve the same clients over and over again. It takes less time and energy and is far more profitable for you.*

"Get the First Call"

ALL SERVICE PROVIDERS GAIN OR LOSE THEIR BUSINESS by how they choose to practice their craft.

Consider these examples:

Attorneys who listen intently, prepare well, and solve problems for their clients are in huge demand. They have no competition. They seem to always "get the first call."

Any surgeon earns their reputation by saving lives and healing many people. The stream of patients lining up to hire them is unending. They have no competition. They always get the first call.

A trusted babysitter is golden! They have no competition. As parents, we always reach out to them first.

Your hairdresser, your house painter, your handyman, your dentist, all *may* seem to have competition. But do they actually? You decided a long time ago to hire the best because you've experienced poor service and poor performance in the past. You refuse to hire mediocrity. You've suffered the poor performers. Never again. Through trial and error, you have finally found the best. You know better than to negotiate price with them; you value their good work far too much. You don't want to offend them or hurt their feelings. They practice their craft with skill and care. They have earned your trust and loyalty. You always ask for them first.

One day, your clients will consider you to be one of their true pros. They will call you first, won't they?

Earning client confidence begins by showing respect, exhibiting professionalism, and maintaining total dedication to the individual needs of your clients.

Let's see how our two agents have applied this advice:

Marie's practice grew and grew because of the proper application of her training and her natural loyalty to her clients. New clients called because they had heard from others that Marie knew her stuff. Many already knew what a legendary teacher Marie was in her past professional life. Her reputation preceded her. They came to her because of the wonderful things their close friends had told them about her. Marie never had to work very hard to gain client trust. That came automatically.

Joe's previous career in the manufacturing industry entailed countrywide travel. When he was home on the weekends, he socialized very little. His only friends were in his golf circle and a few people at his club. Slowly, his girls grew up, graduated university, married, and moved away.

Joe's practice grew despite itself. The market was strong, rates were at historic lows, and the demand for housing was huge. He had mastered his scripts and dialogues long ago. He worked ten- to twelve-hour days. He knew how to capitalize on low-interest rates, the growing housing demand, and a severe lack of inventory. The grind for Joe was long, hard, and fruitful. He loved it. He was rising straight to the top, just as he had planned.

As time went by, Joe sensed that he may have presented as distant, unattached, and cold. He was proud of the fact that he alone was the guy who, no matter the casualties, got the job done. Some clients respected his drive and energy. A few called him back on occasion to relist or buy. But not many.

Set Up Your Very Own Database

You will build and maintain your business using a Customer Relationship Management (CRM) program. This is a software program that manages and markets to your very own private database of clients. The proper use of this software is an essential part of any small business and is essential to your success. Some systems even include lead-generation software.

Which system is best for you? Great question. Your managing broker may offer you the software their firm maintains and upgrades. Should your broker not offer this, be sure to ask around your office. Find out what other agents think of different systems on the market. Check out the ease of use and ability to upgrade the system as time goes by.

Once you choose your system, here's how you may want to get started: Grab your cell phone. Pick out the people who know you and who recognize your name and face. These are the people who you know best. They know you, love you, and trust you. You probably feel the same about them. Enter their contact info into your system.

Next is your secondary level of friends. These people know you by face and name, but not to the level as your vital few. They may not trust you yet because they haven't worked with you yet. They don't necessarily want to work with you at any costs. You are not the one they choose first. Not yet.

The third level will be those who will likely remember your name and face, but not much else.

The more information you can enter into your database, the more effective this system will be over time. Birthdays, graduations, marriages. Dig it all up, and get it into one place.

You may find this process arduous, time-consuming, and a pain to implement. It probably is.

Know this: no CRM, no business. Do it now.

Great. You have all your known clients and potential clients in your database. Over time, it will grow tremendously because you fully intend to place anyone in it whom you meet who may need to buy, sell, or invest in real estate.

You have likely learned how to maneuver through your new system a little bit. If not, crawl around inside it some more. Test it. Get used to it. You and your CRM are going to be friends for decades to come.

I once learned a lesson from an older and very successful business-person. He met vendors throughout his career, like divorce attorneys, ministers, handymen, roofers, stonemasons, etc. He realized he might require their services one day and also realized he might never remember their name or their given line of work. So, he lists everyone in his CRM in this manner: Attorney, Divorce, Albert Jones, 212-555-1111.

Or: Stonemason, Bob Davis, 973-555-2222. Or: Doctor, OB-GYN, Missy Graves, 214-555-3333. That way, when his clients asked for a good attorney, or any pro, he would run a quick search for the type of work needed and provide the referral. Boom. Another way to serve your clients.

Now we check in on our make-believe (but actually real) agents.

Initially, Joe and Joanie took the CRM software system from their old company with them. Most of the names from the old system were useless, as a large majority of customers were commercial.

The advantage of adapting their old system to the new business meant Joe and Joanie saved time, energy, and money. They began to add their network of new clients to the old system immediately. Joanie intended to fully evaluate the real estate-related CRMs and then switch over when the choice had been made.

She realized that the faster they let their list of trusted friends and professionals know about their career change, the faster they would grow their business. They also knew that the new real estate CRMs had been specifically designed for the industry. It not only managed their client list but would also automatically market and send vital information on a consistent basis. When they finally switched over to the new system, Joanie dived right in. Piece of cake. Almost overnight, it provided a daily work list for each of them to organize and prioritize their day and provide sophisticated lead-generation systems.

Marie was introduced to her team's database on her first week. She brought her old system from school. It included contact information of her school network, including former students as well as their parents. With some effort, and with the help of some wonderful whiz kids, it all finally transferred over to the team database. Marie learned some very important secrets from this process. All that time and effort she'd spent over the years maintaining contact information and details on each child and their families had been like a gold mine to her new business.

TIP: *Update your database at least once a year. Correct, remove, and add information.*

TRAP: *Get used to using your database each day. Not taking the time to maintain your database will cripple your growth.*

Other Agents Are Your Partners, Not Your Competition

We all know that you must always represent the best interests of your client. That's the law. Sellers and buyers sometimes like to have their agents negotiate on their behalf. Some of our clients actually love for you to go to battle for them! They expect you to initiate controversy, prolong issues, and be tough on their behalf. This is why most deals won't close without skilled agents from both sides running the show. Professional friendships pay off for everyone involved.

Obviously, when you start in this business, few agents will know of you, and fewer still will really care. Why should they?

You must change this. Your future depends on it. Why? Because agents, being human, will naturally gravitate to agents they know and like. They may not even realize it, but if they know and trust that you will follow through professionally, they will seek you out at every opportunity.

Bust your tail to meet as many of your fellow agents as possible, as quickly as possible. Look for any opportunity to speak with another agent in your market. Do so in person when possible—avoid email and texting when you can. We all know and appreciate that emailing (and to a far greater extent, texting), saves us all hours and hours of work and extra effort.

Texting is simple and fast, but, often, the recipient may misconstrue the message. Texting can and will kill your deals and relationships. Avoid texting when you are attempting to bond with your clients or other agents.

People bond with people, not texts. People remember people who make them smile or laugh. People react to professionals who treat them like professionals. These agents may (or may not) choose to show and sell your listings. If they don't know you now, why do you think a text will do the trick? You must charm your way into their memory.

You must prove to each individual agent you meet that you are a person who should be taken seriously.

Make it your goal to meet one new agent a week face to face. Call top agents in your area. Invite them to coffee. You pay. Introduce yourself, and simply visit. Ask them all about themselves. When it's over, they should walk away pleased with the fact that they took the time to meet you. You will prove to them that they have made a new ally in a brutal business. They will feel flattered you asked to meet with them. It's unlikely other agents have ever asked them to coffee. They will appreciate your efforts.

Over time, you will experience the benefits of these meetings. Deals will be easier to negotiate and problems easier to solve when any two agents know and respect each other.

Tough deals require highly skilled agents. You will find that there are more tough deals than easy ones. Each deal will arrive with its own set of issues and surprises. That's primarily why we have a job.

When other agents know that you practice as a true professional, they will beat a path to your listings. They will go out of their way to return your calls and texts. They will listen to your side of any issue and find ways to work things out. Your sales volume and closings will go up.

Here's another result of good professional relationships: Agents will go way out of their way to seek you out when a new listing comes up. They will call you and tell you before even speaking to the other agents in their own office. Be magic to your fellow agents. They will be calling you . . . or not. Be the person they call first.

The opposite of this is also true. Agents are naturally wary of agents they don't know. It takes more time and energy to bring deals together and hold them together. Further, if you have a reputation as a broker who fails to follow up, replies in text message only, fails to return calls, and doesn't negotiate professionally, you will soon be blackballed from your group. Such sloppy business practices may doom your career.

How you choose to practice on a daily basis creates an impression on others about you. Strive to be that agent most other agents respect, trust, and seek out. Your future depends on it.

Joe suspected that many agents in his market didn't know all about him yet. They would soon learn. He was becoming a force in this business! He was far more talented than the others. He worked so much harder than any of those others. He never missed the monthly and annual awards banquets. He welcomed all the attention. He waved and smiled at the crowd as he walked down the aisle. Top producers surely are looked upon with great reverence, aren't they?

Joe figured that, since Joanie had her license, she could handle the agents on the other side of their deals. As the rainmaker, he felt it was beneath him to deal with the minor details, like appraisals, surveys, or inspections. Spending time with other agents was a total waste for Joe. He'd negotiate directly with another agent when Joanie couldn't, but this seemed so trivial to him.

Marie made a concerted effort to get active in her local real estate association. She volunteered to work on specific committees where she could meet many of her fellow agents. It took years to get know others, but she enjoyed the friendship and fellowship. There were many wonderful people from other agencies, and she looked forward to cultivating relationships everywhere she went.

When she took on a project, she always followed through. She kept others apprised of situations and was naturally easy to be around. She made sure to speak personally (and often) with each agent she did deals with. Marie gained a reputation among her fellow agents as well-organized, demanding at times, kind, and trustable.

Word got out. She knew how to take on challenges and perform admirably. The friends she made and fun times they had were special. Other agents found her approachable, friendly, committed, and at ease with herself. Agents looked forward to working with her. She looked forward to working with them. Marie's practice grew and grew.

Over time, Marie was taught lessons by a few agents. She saw that they were hard to reach, exhausting to negotiate with, or responded by email and text only. Their paperwork was incorrectly filled out or missing entire critical documents. They offered little in the way of professional courtesy. They were combative and sometimes rude.

Marie's duty was to her clients first and foremost. It was her job to ethically and professionally disclose to her clients that these types of agents could prove to be troublesome should they accept a contract from them. They might offer more trouble and pain than any value they may bring to a transaction.

When appropriate for her clients' needs, Marie made a point to show the properties of the agents she personally knew, had good experience with, and whom she knew negotiated in good faith.

Marie did not realize it at the time, but her life was getting easier and more fulfilling. Professional friendships were blossoming for Marie. Bonds that would last her entire career were formed. Lots and lots of sales were to come her way in the future.

Joe's listings sold when the market was red-hot. Joe chose to spend little time working with other agents. That was left to Joanie. When a major problem arose, Joe dived right in, assessed the situation, and if he could, bulldozed his way to a closing. "Whatever it takes to win" became his personal credo.

TIP: *Other agents in your market should know you. They should smile to themselves when they hear your name.*

TRAP: *Agents avoid other agents they find to be unprofessional or who seem hurried or self-important. Always remember this golden rule of real estate: any agent can find a bucket of reasons not to work with any agent they don't like or respect.*

Build Your Website

Lᴉᴋᴇ ᴛʜᴇ CRM ꜱᴏꜰᴛᴡᴀʀᴇ, you can choose from template sites that your office already has in place. Or you can go to the gurus in your city who specialize in premium website development and hosting. You can also work with web-design agencies online or in person and leave all the designing and hosting up to them.

Check around your office. Each agent will likely have their preferred vendors. Go online. See what you find when you check out the websites of the top agents in your market. Pretend you're moving to another city when you study their sites. What makes them attractive to you? Are they easy to navigate? What kind of information do they offer? What pages would you take out? Who produced the site? Can you contact them to see if they can work for you?

Think strategically when you develop your site. Potential clients MUST want to "call you first." They want only what's best for them, right? Your site will prove that you can deliver. Here's why: Because you're going to prove that you will place their needs and desires before all others. You will also prove you can get the job done. You will provide a clear path for them to attain their goals. They will soon see themselves working with you and you alone.

Third-party testimonials will make the most impact for you. You may be brand-new and lack any real experience yet. Ask friends in your business circle to step up for you and talk you up to others. In Marie's case, it may be a former colleague or principal who provides the good news. It doesn't have to be about real estate; it can be about her character, her past awards, her past leadership, etc. Ideally, testimonials should illustrate stellar performance from your immediate past work.

When you ask for testimonials, you will call people who know you, love you, and trust you. They will be more than happy to share their opinions. Some agents have a different approach; with their client's permission, they write the testimonial and send it to the client for approval. That way, they control the narrative and the results. Simply ask for permission to write your own testimonial, provide it to them for approval, and boom!

Joanie chose a web designer and host who specialized in developing and hosting real estate agent websites. She found them online by searching for luxury agent websites in other cities.

She realized that most successful luxury agents don't waste money on weak or unprofessional websites. She soon found many websites from all over the U.S. She located the designer/host and contacted them. Worked like a charm.

Since Marie had joined a team, she plugged her pictures and bio right into an already-up-and-running system. Boom again! She hit the ground running.

TIP: *Your website must be quick to load, easy to navigate, and complete for the market you are trying to serve.*

TRAP: *Consumers will move on quickly when they feel your site is not going to serve them the way they expect it to.*

Here It Is Again— Lead Generation!

LEAD GEN IS THE HEART AND SOUL of any industry, not just real estate.

Lead gen must be the heart and soul of yours. No clients, no business.

It is now time to introduce yourself to your market. Your CRM is up and running. Your website is complete.

Stand up at your desk. Put a smile on your face. Place your first call. "I just called to let you know that I saw your name come up and thought I'd reach out and say 'Hi.'"

Remember, your initial calls are going to people who already know you. They respect and appreciate you from the past. They already know some of the value you bring to the table for them. They will smile when you offer something of value to THEM. This call is all about them, and you're here to prove it. You've entered the residential real estate field, and they need to be aware of it because of the benefits you will bring to THEM. This call is not about you and your new career.

That's what lead generation will be about for you. When you carve out each business day to lead generate, you're merely indicating to your clients that you care about them. You're checking in with them to ask about their family, their work, how they spent their holiday, etc. Talk to them about their dreams. Each contact you make is for real, and its only focus is on your clients, their needs, and their desires. Don't be shy; arrive willing to help your clients in any way you can, regardless of whether their needs have anything to do with buying or selling a home.

Over time, you will uncover where your best clients are likely to come from. Many will come from your personal list of names and addresses that you have built through the years (your CRM). Others may come from lists you buy on the Internet. More will come from working open houses. Some will come from family or friends. Many may come from other forms of lead generation. (More on this later.)

It's now time to learn "lead generation on steroids." Learn this right now. Never forget it. Your very best NEW clients are sent to you by your past satisfied clients. New clients who are sent to you by past clients arrive with full trust in you. They automatically feel they know you because their friend referred them. Pure gold. Nothing better in this life. They've just become the LEAST expensive new client you ever were gifted. Just think—because you chose to practice like the pro you are, an old client remembered you and referred you. All because you cared, you looked out for their best interests. You fought for them. This is how you build a practice.

Joe began to build his business from his pals at the club. They had known each other for years, and his buddies appreciated Joe's drive and desire to win. Actually, a few guys used him because they didn't know anyone else. At least they knew him, sort of . . .

Another way Joe grew his business was by purchasing leads online. He realized that today's home buyers begin their search for their next home online. He would require training to nurture these leads and turn them into clients.

Joanie found training videos for Joe on YouTube. He learned the scripts and dialogues. He practiced and practiced. Joe hung in there. Soon, Joe began closing on his leads. Joe got busy. He applied his superior sales skills and racked up closings in only a matter of months. The market in his town was red-hot. Interest rates were at all-time lows. Buyers and sellers seemed to be everywhere. Joe considered himself an overnight success. This was almost like shooting fish in a barrel.

Joanie kept Joe focused. They were cashing in on high demand and low supply for houses. Joe worked like a dog, remained in the grind, and moved up the sales volume charts. He was so excited. Joe was crushing this business!

"Get 'em in, get 'em out, get 'em closed," he would say.

His past corporate life had taught him this. He had turned his old sales group into nationally prominent performers. Their relationships were all business. They knew how to schmooze and entertain, but at the end of the day, it was all business. He had enjoyed success in the past by winning bids, delivering decent quality, and providing a decent "post-sale" communication network.

"This new real estate gig should be just like my old job," thought Joe. What Joe failed to perceive was that home listings and sales were highly personal, family-oriented endeavors. He failed to recognize that he was moving moms, dads, kids, and pets—not houses.

Volume of transactions was the key for Joe. Close 'em. Move on to the next one.

Joanie managed each home sale or purchase with business-like professionalism and skill. She faced each set of inevitable issues with poise. Their volume of sales was tremendous. She found that she had little time to develop personal relationships with clients or other agents. Their volume was too great. They were cranking it out, and she had to keep up.

Joe let her handle all this personal stuff with clients. He approached each sale in a very clinical manner. He was very talented and said what he thought were all the right things. He moved quickly, leaving little time for small talk. Bonding was not part of this equation for him. He was the rainmaker, after all. Agents remembered Joanie as a professional, but they hardly knew Joe. He'd step in to manage crisis situations and save a deal, but the strong market was on his side. He played hardball almost every time. Agents never forgot Joe, but for all the wrong reasons.

Clients came away generally mildly satisfied with Joe's job performance. They never really bonded with Joe; he seemed far too busy for that sort of thing. He'd developed a reputation for sales volume. He was hard-charging, but he wasn't good at building and maintaining relationships. He had no time for the warm-and-fuzzy stuff. He felt that his past successes did not require bonding, building trust, or professional friendships. Client feelings took a back seat. He felt that he didn't need or expect loyalty from his clients or other agents. He had new clients coming out of his ears. The Internet delivered hundreds of them on a daily basis.

Wow! Just think—he had moved into the top-ten producers in his town . . . in such a short time. Joe felt very good about himself at this stage of his career. He walked with a swagger.

Meanwhile, Joe's daughters left for college in other states. They came home for Thanksgiving and Christmas but spent summers abroad or in summer session. Joe bought each of them brand-new cars. It was the least he could do for them.

Across town, Marie took her buyer's representation classes very seriously. She dotted all the I's and crossed the T's. She learned how to lead generate. She went to all the local and state training classes she could. She socialized with agents from other companies and made good friends. Her skill level expanded. Her confidence grew. Most of her initial business came from her past students, mostly *their* parents. She began to make good money. Her clients bragged about her to their friends. She and her team could flat-out *deliver!* It was always fun to work with Marie and her group. All her old clients could not wait to send her new home buyers and sellers.

Marie came to appreciate the fact that she worked with a dedicated team. They were obviously well trained and practiced as true professionals. They went out of their way to help her, answer her many questions, and make her feel welcome. They showed the same care and concern for their clients' best interests that she did. Marie had truly lucked into a great work situation.

When homes sell within the first few days on the market, people begin to pay attention. Marie worked with home buyers, and they often were placed in multiple offer situations. There were lots of buyers chasing too few listings. Prices were rising, and buyers were becoming frustrated. She learned that some of her clients were growing anxious and were pushing her to buy homes that were marginal at best. Marie began to preach patience to her clients. She learned how to defend and protect her clients from buying trouble.

She stressed to her clients the importance of home inspections, property surveys, and disclosure statements. Her curiosity seemed endless. She wanted to know everything discovered in due diligence and how it might affect her clients. Over time, she learned how to spot potential trouble and point it out to her clients. She urged her clients to purchase conservatively. She knew that, one day, she would be asked to resell the homes her clients were buying now. Poorly built or maintained homes would not resell well. Her experience evolved into wisdom. Marie's reputation as an excellent buyer's agent was growing.

TIP: *Lead generation is your future. Embrace it.*

TRAP: *When you have no leads, the results are no listings, no buyers, and no business.*

Old McDonald Had a Farm.
So Must You.

Your farm will become your mecca for lead generation.

You may have heard of farming by now. A farm is usually a geographic area of concentration that agents spend hours of their attention on. This area may be a large condominium complex of four hundred units, a neighborhood of 250 homes, or perhaps a zip code. Your job is to become the agent of choice for the families who live in your farm.

Here's what exceptional agents do to build their farms: They may choose to develop their farm in one large neighborhood and never step outside of it. They know everyone and everything that goes on in their farm. Their goal is to become so dominant in their farm that they don't have to look elsewhere for business. Their strategy is genius.

Experienced agents know which neighborhoods turn over the most. This becomes their farm.

They are active in their church, community, or schools. They choose one or two groups and then set about to truly excel in developing strong relationships.

You might describe these as civic or church-group farms. A successful agent will work hard to be the person who can be counted on to get any job done—and done well. If it's fundraising, they kill it; if it's planning a picnic, they outshine. Their reputation for excellence grows and grows. People in their farm grow to trust and count on them. Heck, if they do such a great job in our civic club, they must really be good in real estate!

A great agent will know everything there is to know about their farm. If it's a high-rise condo, they know everyone who lives there. They memorize names and faces, and learn to be helpful and gracious. They know the management company; they make it a point to become friends with each of the members of the HOA (Homeowners Association). They know the little old lady who lives in the penthouse. They know the name of the dog that lives in unit #306. They know the influencers, the movers and shakers, the troublemakers, the peacemakers, and where all the bodies are buried. They avoid conflict, except when absolutely necessary. When there is any activity, they are right there in the middle of it. They know all the best vendors, the plumbers, the interior decorators, the electricians, the contractors, the hardware-store people down the street, the doctors, the attorneys, the local government officials. They get problems solved for people. They drive people to the doctor. They are known within the group as peacemakers and fierce protectors of their "family."

Over time, an exceptional agent becomes part of the fabric of their farm. They are considered an indispensable asset to everyone who lives there. Homeowners love to see an exceptional agent take an active role in protecting a neighborhood or enhancing its appeal.

Loyalty and trust are the result. Home buyers and sellers prefer to work with active, well-connected agents.

Some believe it takes years to develop this kind of gravitas, this kind of respect, this kind of power. Perhaps. A true pro just dives right in! They meet the movers and shakers. They begin to understand the politics and the pitfalls of taking sides. They look for ways to solve problems. They look for ways to serve and improve people's lives.

The exceptional agent becomes THE go-to guy. Someone everyone can trust. They are the agent clients always "Call First."

Here are some things to consider when choosing your farm.

1. Choose a geographic area of strong turnover. There needs to be plenty of sellers.
2. Choose well-built, well-maintained homes.
3. Choose a vibrant community (or one that is clearly on the way back up in preference).
4. Choose a neighborhood of historically upward trends.
5. Where applicable, make sure there is a strong and healthy HOA. Neighborhood HOAs that suffer lawsuits and poor dues collections should be avoided.
6. Test scores in the public schools should be excellent.
7. Hospitals, shopping, entertainment, dining, and the arts must be accessible.
8. Values should be upwardly moving, or, at the very least, stable. It helps if they are trending up.
9. Taxation should be stable.
10. The local government should be conservative and stable.
11. Crime rates should be low.
12. Drive times to major employment centers are accepted by most families as a given fact.

13. Great public transportation is a huge plus, though not required in some areas.
14. Make sure you choose a farm that is geographically close to where you live.

Perhaps you wish to develop your farm and your business around specific and unique communities. Let's say you live in a vacation-resort area, a good size retirement community, or a large co-op in New York City. How about a gated community? Perhaps luxury is your cup of tea. Each of these may serve as an excellent choice; just make sure there is enough turnover to make the kind of living you want.

Joe chose two farms. The first was his immediate neighborhood. Many of the neighbors at least knew of him. Joanie could saturate and market the area with ease. His second and most important farm became the online leads he bought. There were now companies that specialized in attracting, nurturing, and developing home buyers and sellers. The leads from these companies were expensive and worth it to Joe. If there was one thing he had learned, it was how to develop and close on a cold prospect.

Marie developed her first farm from the kids and parents of those she had taught over the past twenty years. It was slow-going at first, but it wasn't long before buyers and sellers came to her on a consistent basis. Marie knew most of the home builders, many of the city-council people, as well as the mayor. She and her family attended a local church. She was active in and served on community boards. Over time, as people discovered Marie was now in real estate, they recalled her first-class teaching skills. They recalled how she made them feel special when she taught them. They almost jumped at the chance to work with her when they found out she was now buying and selling homes. In fact, they chose to call her first.

TIP: *A properly developed farm is the gold standard of any real estate practice. Like a real farm, it takes time, skill, and devotion to develop and pay off.*

TRAP: *Be clever in your choice of a farm. Go where the sales are.*

Work-Life Balance and You . . .

. . . and your business . . . and your family
. . . and your health . . . and . . . and . . . and . . .

Let's get real here for a minute. Does "life balance" exist in the real world? Yes and no. That's up to you.

As you'll find with any new career, when you first begin in real estate, you will feel like a firehose has been placed in your mouth and turned on. There won't be enough time to take it all in. All you may want to do is learn, learn, and learn some more. This may push other important things off your plate, like your home life, your partner, or your children. Your sanity and physical health will likely suffer.

Don't fall for it. Things will be wonky some days and probably some weeks and months. This comes with *any* new job. Here's where you've got to struggle to maintain balance.

Schedule time for maintaining your mental and physical health. It takes energy to build your business. Set parameters and expectations with your clients right up front. Tell them what to expect from you and what you expect from them. Tell them that your phone remains "off" during evening hours, when you are in meetings, and especially when you have family obligations. They must know and respect that your policy is to not answer texts, emails, or phone calls until you've finished your other obligations.

Set appointments for each aspect of your daily life. Life balance is not likely to take place for you unless you set these appointments and KEEP them. Organize your written schedule ahead of time. Appreciate that your appointments include lead generation, workouts at the gym, kids' school events, even naps. Vacations and time off are key to recharging and maintaining your edge.

Clients will appreciate and welcome the boundaries you set as well as the fact that you make your intentions clear to them. They will respect that you manage your life well. Clients realize that, when you are organized in one area of your life, you usually are organized in the rest of it. They realize that you know what you're doing and have everything under control; they relax, and you both get to have a much more enjoyable experience.

We all know that Joe had chosen to conquer the world of real estate. Joanie had his schedule totally planned each day to lead generate, list, and sell real estate. That is all. As time went on, Joe became far too busy to play golf, too busy to help out at church. Vacations with his family were sometimes canceled to meet with the CEO who was flying into town on short notice. The wife and girls went on without him. They would get over it, he figured. They should realize that the money he was making was what sent them to Hawaii. He knew they would love that. Joe may have missed some stuff, but that was okay with him. He was becoming known as a force in real estate. The Mac Daddy. He would relax later.

During her teaching career, Marie learned to work from a written plan. This plan included scheduling daily, weekly, and monthly activities. Marie handled her clients like she handled her students. She made clear what she expected from them and what they could expect from her. Her clients soon came to learn and respect the way she did business.

Marie also scheduled her life outside of real estate. She spent time at the gym and time with friends. She set appointments to relax and rejuvenate. It was right there on her schedule. She rarely missed these appointments. She'd found out years ago that when she wrote it down, it got done. Work-life balance for Marie was easy. Everything was written on her calendar. Everything.

The result for Marie and her family was that she was far more prepared, relaxed, and focused.

As a real estate newbie, your first year or so will likely be out of balance. Some days or weeks will be massively out of balance. It's okay. The education you must take in and the time and energy required to get things going will be substantial. Remember to take full advantage of every single thing your brokerage offers in the way of training. Pay the price now. You will not regret it. I offer a little secret at this point: schedule and commit to at least one full day off every two weeks. Become watchful and protective of your time. When you wake up each morning exhausted and grumpy, it's time to reassess and rebalance. It's time to regroup and recharge.

TIP: *Work-life balance is a very good thing.*

TRAP: *Expect your work and life to often be far out of balance and wacky for the first few years. It's going to happen. The goal is to return to it as soon as possible.*

Surround Yourself with Quality People

W E ALL KNOW THIS TYPE OF PERSON. They hang around the coffee machine sipping and exchanging war stories. The stories usually revolve around their problems. There always seems to be an issue with their real estate practice. You know who these people are. They exist in every company and in all walks of life. Time is passing, and the clock is ticking for them. You already know that their sales and their attitude toward success . . . suck. Do not try to save these guys. It's not your job. Your job is to build and protect your future. Smile and greet everyone with a "good morning!"

Keep your eyes and ears open in your office. You will soon find out where the high-volume winners hang out. Go there. Find ways to be of service to them. They will naturally pick up on the fact that you intend to be successful.

Let's talk about your own real estate team now. You must assemble your professional "full service" real estate team as soon as possible. These are the vendors who support your sales and marketing efforts.

Align yourself with vendors who think like you do, ones that provide first-class service, charge a fair price, and enjoy a fine reputation. Your team will include your lender, home inspector, surveyor, CPA, closing attorney, handyman, and general contractor. It is NOT composed of rookies. Your team is "the best of the best." That's why you've brought them on, after all. The work they perform is, in fact, tied directly to you. Never forget that.

Referring a top-notch vendor means their experience and wisdom will pay off for your clients and you. Develop and maintain rock-solid relationships with your team of vendors. They are another part of your value proposition. In due time, your clients will make you the First Call when the plumbing goes bad, the roof leaks, or the house smells. You want that call! It provides you the opportunity to reacquaint yourself and help your clients out. They will come to depend on you and you alone. Boom.

Expect your real estate team to refer lots of business to you. Remind them every once in a while. They will if you ask them.

Marie's past career taught her that she had made some of her best friends in the teachers' lounge. She naturally gravitated to like-minded teachers, and they had become fast friends. These guys were naturally happy and successful. When she joined her real estate team, she found some of those same type people. Marie's vendor group was fully in place when she joined her team. They had all been working together for years and years. Marie inherited the tremendous gift of vendors who cared about their clients as well as the quality of their work. They became her work family. She seemed to fit right in. What a great advantage for Marie! Her client list grew and grew.

Joe had no idea where the break room was. Joanie had a press pot ready for him on his desk each morning. Joe never walked down the hall to his office. He ran.

He totally depended on Joanie to handle all vendors. Joe rarely made any contact with them. Joe didn't see the vendors as part of his value proposition. He held himself above all of that. Joe expected Joanie to get any issues solved quickly and without causing a problem for him. He demanded each vendor "snap to" when called. He felt they needed him. He did not need them.

TIP: *Hang with winners only. Stop watching the news. They sell fear and foster depression.*

TRAP: *Victims find a way to blame it all on others. You are not a victim and never will be.*

Your Ace in the Hole:
An Advisory Board

Speaking of "the best of the best," it is now time to set up your personal advisory board. Your board will be made up of people you respect. If you respect them, chances are others in your community do, too. These men and women will likely come from all walks of life and various industries; they will offer wise counsel to you and your group. Host a monthly or quarterly breakfast. Maintain the same agenda each time. Offer new updates on your local market. Offer general insights on the market as well as your expectations for the upcoming year. Always show them that you are on top of "all things real estate." Always offer something of value to them. Something they can take away and make money with. The rewards you bring to them should be rich and diverse. Wonderful discussions and debates will occur. They will look forward to attending. Business and friendships will blossom. Referrals will happen. Your business will grow.

TIP: *Advisors enjoy being advisors. Be curious. Learn from them.*

TRAP: *Don't drop the ball. Stay in touch monthly with your board. Keep the group alive and vibrant. Provide stimulating accounts of the business success of others in other fields.*

The Tax Man Cometh
and Remaineth Permanently

WE ALL REALIZE WE MUST PAY our fair share in taxes. What you may fail to realize is that, as an independent contractor, you pay taxes four times a year. Each quarter of each year for the Rest. Of. Your. Life.

The IRS is not an organization you can say you forgot or overlooked. The penalties are brutal. It is simply not worth getting that letter itemizing your fines and penalties.

Know this: The attorneys at the IRS sit around all day with their feet on the desk, waiting on the call to come after you. Yummy! They slide their feet off their desk, lean forward in the chair, and lick their chops. You are about to star on an episode of Shark Week . . . and you are not the shark.

The good news here is that, when you find and hire a savvy CPA, they fully intend to see that you never miss a payment. They will nag you (as your parents once did), until you pay Uncle Sam "on time, every time." You may hate this, but sooner or later, you will have to accept it.

Good news: An exceptional CPA will see that you take every legal deduction available. They will happily illustrate ways to save on taxes that you've never thought of. That's why you pay them. Remember that you must provide accurate records of your business. Demand and keep accurate records. They will serve as the backbone and structure for the work your CPA does, as well as help you manage your growing business.

Joe had no clue about taxes. Luckily, Joanie did. She kept meticulous records. When they became agents, Joanie brought her old software over as a stopgap. There were better systems for independent businesses, and she knew it. Before long, she got things the way she wanted. Joe had no idea how wonderful she was. Soon, she produced monthly statements and saw to it that he never missed paying his taxes. Where did Joe find this superstar anyway?

Marie set her new business accounting system up after seeking out the knowledge and experience of other brokers. She also checked with her CPA. Her early real estate training taught her to run her new business . . . like a business. All business funds remained separate and apart from her family's. They never commingled. He advised her on the proper use of her software bookkeeping system and helped her get up and running. Soon Marie learned to read and understand her monthly balance sheet and Profit and Loss statement. Marie felt in control of this part of her business. Each month's reports provided a snapshot of her business. She kept her expenses in line, as well as charted her income goals. This reduced Marie's stress. She slept well knowing her exact numbers.

How Old Millionaires Got That Way

Few, if any, practicing agents have ever been offered this sage advice.

An old real estate multimillionaire once whispered to his agents, "You must always remember that you make your money when you BUY real estate, not when you sell it." True story.

There are several reasons this maxim is true. The first is that you must become savvy enough to judge the nature and vibe of any local market in which you intend to invest. You must ask enough questions to properly judge the property as well as the listing agent. You absolutely must judge the seller's reasons for selling in the first place. You must have ALL the empirical data you can find on the future of the area. You must know the local politics, the local power base. Is the area moving down in condition and popularity or on the way back from tough times? How is the employment, education, and crime data? Is there pride of ownership evident? Do people take good care of their property? If it's a rental area, how are the rental rates doing? Is the neighborhood junky, trashy, or run-down? Are there five cars parked in the front yard? Is the overall situation going up or down? Is the city well-run? Are the taxes going up or down? Perhaps there is a local or national calamity going on—a major employer shutting down, a flood, a fire, an earthquake, a massive recession, ultra-high interest rates, or perhaps the local market has simply taken a breather.

All successful professional real estate investors and their agents perform due diligence and more. They talk to people at the close-by gas stations. They hang a bit in the local coffee shop. They know the "lay of the land." They discover why people who live in the immediate area enjoy it or wish they could live elsewhere.

Sometimes a property is brought to market, and the reason for the sale is not about the money. It may be about business or family circumstances. Timing could somehow be a critical issue. Be prepared to move fast.

Perhaps the market is in shambles. Everyone is selling out. There is panic in the streets (like 2007 or 2020). That is exactly the time the smart money emerges. Your investor has cash and is ready to close . . . at the right price. Your investor is mature and sophisticated. They realize when it is time to pull the trigger.

Here's another good example. A decade or so ago, our city suffered a flood of epic proportions. Thousands of homes that had never suffered water damage went underwater. Many homeowners didn't have flood insurance. They felt they did not need it, as their home was considered out of the flood plain, and lenders did not require it.

Unfortunately, many homeowners did not have the savings to repair their homes. Some simply walked away and let the banks have them. The result was that hundreds of homes and condominiums were sold for virtually pennies on the dollar. Slowly, investors purchased, repaired, and rebuilt. Renters were the first to return to the newly renovated properties. Federal flood maps were rewritten after this occurrence, yet hundreds and hundreds of homes that flooded were still not included in the maps. Investors who were willing to take a small chance held on for a few years. That's all it took. New families moved to town who had never heard of the flood. Many old-timers simply forgot about it. No floods had taken place since 2010. Most of the affected homes had been removed or rebuilt. Original values returned. Investors took a chance, and it paid off massively for them. They had to be prepared to buy flooded-out homes, rebuild or repair them, hold them for years as rentals, and ultimately sell at substantial gains. That's why they are called investors. You win some, you lose some.

Here's how you spot a great investor: They will make offers that are well-received by the sellers and that close on time. They will develop a reputation and track record for integrity. They know how to pay far less than market price because they've worked far harder than the rest. They leverage market timing and conduct highly skilled negotiations. If you are well-schooled in analyzing markets and determining the value of investment properties, you must seek out and work with seasoned investors. Always seek out the pros. The training and education required by you to school rookie investors is not going to make you any money. It will only cost you time, energy, and money.

You may not be a pro yet, but with time and lots of good training, you will get there. Should you be interested in this part of real estate, find those old pros who have made all that money. Work under them if you can. Bring tremendous value to them somehow. This will pay off for you. Become the agent they highly value and the one they always "Call First."

Here's what Joe did. His market was, of course, high-flying and red-hot. The inventory of luxury homes was low. There was not much to choose from, and if his buyers wanted to move to his town, they needed to make decisions quickly. He pushed his luxury buyers to pounce quickly. He used his scripts and dialogues to scare many home buyers into buying homes that were, in fact, not in the best locations, the best condition, or very well-built or well-maintained. As you might imagine, it finally caught up to him. More on this later.

Marie's skill as a buyer's representative grew gradually with each client. She attended all inspections. She asked loads of questions and asked inspectors to point out things to look for as signs of danger to her clients before they presented or negotiated a contract. She saved her clients tons of time, money, and heartache. They came to value her skills and her upfront and honest opinions. She made it clear to each client that, although she was not a home inspector, she had seen certain issues in the past and found them troublesome. They may have to look a bit harder and a bit longer, but Marie fought defensively for her clients.

Her reputation grew and grew as a conservative buyer's rep, one who defended her clients' best interests. It wasn't about the money for Marie; it was about finding and buying the best homes in the best locations, and at a price that reflected the nature of the expenditures she felt her clients would have to make to bring the property up to neighborhood standards.

TIP: *Remain curious throughout your career.*

TRAP: *Dropping out of sight from this particular business for weeks or months at a time will cause you huge grief. It takes too much time to catch up.*

Exceptional Agents Exhibit Exceptional Product Knowledge

Unless things have really changed lately, real estate schools are required to spend little time, if any, teaching new agents how a home is built or maintained. There are few or no questions on the national or state exams related to the subject.

Think about this for a minute. Each medical school student must spend the first few years devoted to the intense study of the entire human body. They must prove their total knowledge before moving on in their training. Each pre-med student will be provided their own cadaver, and at some point, dissect it part by part, becoming intimately familiar with the entire body. After months of study, learning, and passing tests, they can move on with their schooling.

Same thing goes for a plumber or an electrician. Strict laws surround the training and testing of new candidates. Our society demands and expects it. Applicants for their license exams may need to first pass formal training in an accredited school. Future plumbers then spend four years serving as an apprentice before being granted a journeyman's license to practice. Four years. For future electricians, even more extended training is required to obtain a Master Electrician's designation.

You will be different from the herd. You will develop and maintain an *intimate knowledge* of how homes are constructed in your area. Just like any well-trained med student or plumber or electrician, you will know *every tiny detail* of a well-built home. You will learn how to apply your rare skill to each individual home sale or purchase. This wisdom and knowledge will set you miles apart from other agents. Your clients will appreciate and depend on your skills. They will talk about you to others, telling them how you protected them and guided them to their lovely well-built or -maintained new home. You will be held in reverence and respect. You will become the agent people refer and "Call First."

Marie knew how to study and prepare. She introduced herself to new-home sales agents and asked them to take her on tours of their inventory. She asked to see homes in all stages of the build cycle. From footings to roofs, she learned how well-built houses were constructed and maintained. She also learned critical information about the most popular floor plans. She soon realized that the large national builders spent many hundreds of thousands of dollars on market research. This research had led to the designs and specifications that appeal to home buyers the most. She used this knowledge to advise her buyers on what's hot, as well as her sellers on the trends that most impressed home buyers. She was making herself invaluable to her clients.

Yeah, yeah, yeah. Joe knew all about houses. People liked them, or they didn't. He had realized a while back that buyers had to hustle to even get in line to bid on almost any home. The pressure was on them. Sellers rarely cared much to really "gussy up" their home to sell it. They didn't have to. There were eight to ten buyers for every home that came onto the market. Joe was familiar with all the scripts and dialogues it took to close on new listings. He also used his skills to herd buyers into homes that were marginal in condition or location. This had become a numbers game for Joe.

TIP: *Continued education is critical to any profession. Welcome it.*

TRAP: *Construction techniques and materials are changing each year. Your clients will expect you to prove that you are updated on the latest. If you fail to deliver the knowledge they demand, they may move on.*

Chapter 29

Avoid Buying
"A Pig in a Poke"

"A PIG IN A POKE" IS AN OLD SOUTHERN TERM that gained popularity when farmers would buy livestock sight unseen . . . and get bamboozled.

When you are a buyer's agent and you drive up to a home and look at it from the outside, you should be able to spot some deal-killers right off the bat. Does the roof sag? Are there obvious and large cracks in the exterior walls? Is there standing water in the basement, crawl space, or cellar? Where does all that water go in a storm? Are there stains on the roof? How's the paint job? Are there storm windows? Are there cracks in the interior walls? Is the landscaping out of control or nonexistent? What is the condition of the driveway? Is the yard sloppy, or is it well-kept? How about the neighbors? Do they show pride in their homes? Are there more rentals than homeowners? Renters are not known for maintaining properties like homeowners. You can usually spot a neighborhood of rentals by the overall condition of the buildings and grounds.

Here's where you step in. Should your client be a flipper or a rehab specialist, you may have just found a gem. Most of them have suffered and learned from buying poorly in the past.

Should your client be a **first-time buyer**, well, that's a very different story. First-time buyers arrive as **raw rookies**. They rarely know much about home construction, maintenance, or repairs. They may buy that "pig-in-a-poke," a nightmare of a money pit.

As a brand-new agent, no one will expect you to exhibit tremendous product knowledge. That will take time. But the more you close deals, the more you will learn from the pros, your home inspectors!

Perhaps your brokerage will invite a seasoned home inspector to come into the office and offer training. See that you take time to attend. Further, you should **always** be present at each and every home inspection "wrap-up" meeting. This is held at the end of each home inspection. The inspector will show photos of each exception they find. You must remain curious. Ask questions. If you don't understand an issue or think your client may not, ask them to fully explain the issue. Learn. Learn. Learn.

So, what's the big deal? Why should you have to do this? After all, it's the home inspector's job!

The big deal is that, if you spot these deal-killers early on, you can alert your buyers. You'll try to prevent them from falling in love with a money pit, making an offer, inspecting it, and being forced to walk away. The cost to them in terms of time and money is far too high. It's also a cost to you! Your time, your energy, and your money may also be wasted. Think about it for a second—if you actually help them buy "a dog," who will they ultimately blame? You. Learn to buy homes defensively. Learn how to spot deal-killers well before you go to contract.

NOTE: Never fancy yourself as a home inspector. Unless you have the training and possess the license, never act like one. Simply qualify any statement by indicating that you're not a home inspector. Then go on to explain that you've seen homes in the past that were in similar shape, and they ultimately failed to close due to their condition. Make it clear to your clients that any opinions should be verified by a licensed professional. Remember, your legal obligation is always to protect your client and their best interests.

Examples of these easily spotted deal-killers are sagging roofs, major cracks in the foundations and interior walls, or standing water in the crawlspace or basement. Others might include major mold infestations or old, non-functioning plumbing, electrical, or HVAC systems.

Poor construction may be easily spotted, even by people new to the business. Meandering walls, rolling floors, or weird smells. Standing water on the interior of the home. Low water pressure, flickering lights, evidence of animal infestation or piles of waste should be noted to your clients. I'll say this again: You should not pretend to be something you are not. Defer any statements you make to the verification of a professional home inspector.

Should your buyer be a professional flipper, seasoned investor, or have experience maintaining homes of this type in the past, homes with these issues may be exactly what they've hired you to find. Assemble all the problems on a list, and determine the costs to repair or replace the items. Make sure your buyer realizes the commitment they must make in time and energy to bring the property up to their expectations.

TIP: *Proof of your knowledge to your client will result in their respect for you, and they will rely on you from then on.*

TRAP: *Don't ever say anything that you don't know as the Gospel Truth. When you get caught in a misstatement, trust will be lost, and your relationship may be doomed.*

People of Influence and Your Future

You probably already know many of them. Think about that firecracker cashier at your local grocery store. Every shopper in the store loves her. She greets them with a bright smile and calls them by their first names. She is truly a person of influence. She may even know when people are buying or selling in your farm. That bank manager may know some folks. That daycare owner. How about the local president of your Rotary, or Chamber of Commerce, or the head of your PTA? Could it be your city alderman? How about the head of your local real estate investment club?

From the cashier to the mayor, each powerful influencer has risen to the position of leadership within your community because people like them, trust their judgement, and follow them. They have been found to be people who get things done. They are trustable, they take on challenges, and deliver. They seem to know a huge amount of people in their community. These types of people hold huge sway with their wide circle of friends. Should they meet you and like you, they may (or may not) choose to refer you to their trusted friends.

It is obvious that you must develop a healthy relationship with influencers. They know and are respected by lots of folks. When they know and respect you, they will likely refer you.

Know that this process will take time and energy. It will pay off for you. It is a sure-fire way to build your practice and your own personal influence.

TIP: *Just one person of serious influence may, in fact, make your entire career.*

TRAP: *Avoid making enemies whenever possible.*

"Trouble" Is Your Best Friend

I BET NO ONE'S SHARED THIS WITH YOU YET. Trouble can and will be your very best friend. Sometimes the bigger the problem, the better. I am not kidding.

The average real estate sale is touched by thirty-five to fifty individuals. Each deal is dependent on the timely and professional actions of each individual involved.

You may not realize this yet, but it is YOU who's ultimately responsible to see that each of these individuals is doing their job according to the terms of the contract. You must ride herd on **all** of them. The lender, the home inspector, the repair people, the closing people, the zoning people, etc.

Sometimes, one or more of these people will drop the ball. You *will* immediately realize the mistake, because you are on top of each phase of all of your closings. Your clients may never actually know you triaged, but you did. You now have a happy client, you now get paid, and you will likely get several referrals to boot.

But wait . . . more problems are coming!

We all know life happens. Weather, divorce, sick kids, loss of employment, vacations, holidays, and all those other unexpected life situations seem to pop up when we least expect them and right before the deal is set to close. Everything is going along quite nicely until then. Surprise! Crunch! Boom! Collapse of all systems! Hello? Houston, we have a problem. Some agents run for the exits. Not you.

You jump into the phone booth, change into your cape and tights, and save the day! You will look at each crisis with an open mind and sober attitude. Whatever it takes, however long it takes, you will be there for your clients. You will not point fingers or lose your cool. You WILL save the day. This is what you signed up for. This IS your job. Welcome to the world of residential real estate sales.

Most successful agents use systems and checklists to avoid many problems I've just described. Expect your broker to provide this list for you. If they don't have one, make one yourself.

Anticipate at least one issue emerging from every deal, possibly more. Welcome the chance to shine. Welcome the occasion when all seemed lost but you found a way to make it happen! Your reputation as a true professional will grow. They will talk about you. They will spread the word.

Marie taught hormonal teenagers. She learned all about angst and drama. She learned how to spot trouble before it even began. Marie cared about her clients and their families. She realized that "life happens." She prepared her clients for the unexpected in advance. She helped them appreciate that surprises were likely. She met each issue in a timely manner, head on, and with maturity.

Marie learned, over time, how to handle most every unforeseen circumstance. Her magical skills seemed to be baked-in to her practice. It all came easy to Marie. She could stare down a raging bull and hug a sobbing home buyer. It was in her nature.

Marie's professional reputation flourished over time. Buyers and sellers talked about her astonishing skills. Her positive energy and the twinkle in her eye were contagious. Marie's income doubled and tripled in just a few years. Most of her new sales came from referrals from her past clients.

Joe was the "big dog" in town. He sold dozens of homes. He showed little patience for other agents and their lack of preparation or skill. If anyone got in his way, he simply ran over them. The deals kept coming at a furious pace. If some of his deals fell apart, so what? The entire community must realize that he was a top producer! He had become busy and important!

The months and years seemed to pass. Slowly the word about how Joe chose to practice got out. Working with Joe was a challenge, at best. Few people could find a way to make a connection with him. Other agents avoided him. His style was combative and dismissive. Past clients rarely called him. He seemed way too busy to help them. It was easier to call the new agent they'd just met at their kids' summer camp.

Joe never seemed to miss his old clients. Strangers kept moving to town, and his Internet leads kept Joe very busy. He continued to build what he believed was his stellar reputation. He was now listed as one of the top agents in his company.

TIP: *Welcome trouble as your excuse to serve and serve well.*

TRAP: *Avoiding trouble or blaming others for any problem is not a good way to serve your clients or your future.*

You've Got to Know When to Hold 'Em and When to Fold 'Em

LET'S FACE IT. From time to time, you will let your clients down. Sometimes your clients will fail you or fire you. You may sometimes have to fire yourself. Out of nowhere, deals will simply fall apart or blow sky high. You will have lost confidence in your clients, or they in you. You will sense when the time is right. Choose to move on. Save your time, your money, and your energy. Be professional. Be courteous. Be courageous. Simply say, "I'm probably not the agent for you right now." Hold your head high, and leave without regret. You realize you have done everything within your power to represent your clients' best interests. That's all you should worry about. You did your best. It feels very good when you finally do it. I promise.

What about real estate deals? Should some of them fail? Of course. This is another reason you have a job. There will be a point that your client's time, money, and energy are too expensive for you to remain in the deal. Sometimes it will be up to you to help them determine when to fish or cut bait.

Always work toward a win-win for everyone. After all, that's your job. The skill to perform well in this arena may come naturally, or it has to be learned. Strive to become the best negotiator. As you gain skills, your reputation will grow. Other agents and clients will notice.

Occasionally the two parties in any deal may become totally intractable. As due diligence continues, lots of issues may emerge. It may be time to walk away, or not. When you first start out, and before advising your clients to kill any deal, you should seek the advice of your mentor, coach, or managing broker. They have been there many times before. Time and experience will teach you how to spot these deal-killers well before signing contracts and paying for due diligence. You will learn how to guide your clients through this painful process without losing their confidence or respect.

Needless to say, it was important to Joe that he win. Notice that I did not say that he wanted to win for his clients. Joe had learned in his other life how to maneuver and manipulate others. Even his own clients. When it was in Joe's best interest, things seemed to get done. Joe was brought before his board's professional standards group on several occasions. Time and reputation were slowly but surely catching up with him.

Marie had developed a keen "sixth sense" as a teacher. She could tell when her clients were frightened. She responded to her clients the way she responded to her students: upfront, honestly, and with practicality. Together they learned how to assess each issue, negotiate the middle ground, and figure out what was best for all. Sometimes, a buyer or seller would budge a little here or there. Other times, the situations were too much to overcome. Marie would guide each client (and deal) with skill, devotion, and determination. Marie was becoming the consummate real estate professional. Other agents gained respect for her, and her clients loved her. She was becoming the agent people chose to call first.

TIP: *Cut and run when it is clearly time to do so. Your clients will appreciate the confidence and courage you show in protecting them.*

TRAP: *Ambivalence or your lack of resolve will become very apparent to your clients. Learn to act decisively.*

Seasoned Clients Have Been There, Done That

When you first start out, you may be blessed enough to work with clients who have bought or sold homes on more than one occasion. Their past experience will lend a certain maturity to the entire process.

Think about it for a second: If they are experienced home buyers, they won't present with the huge learning curve that first-time buyers have. They are far more focused on the specifics of the type of home they want and the location. They have learned from their past mistakes and successes. They are far more relaxed and focused than brand-new home buyers.

I label experienced buyers and sellers as "The Survivors." Why? Because selling any home is an arduous process. It's a royal pain. The lessons learned by home sellers remain in their memories for decades.

Ask them all about their past experiences. Ask them who their favorite agent was from the past. Ask them about the agent who was not so hot. Ask them to elaborate for you. Be sure to mimic the things the best agent did for them. Avoid doing the things the past sloppy agent did.

When you first start out as a brand-new agent, know that second-third-, and fourth-time buyers have knowledge that you don't yet have. They may ask questions to which they already know the answers. Should you not have a decent answer, say so. Promise to find out and report back. You will win their confidence, and they will remain relaxed and trusting of you.

The manner Marie chose to practice was remarkable because of her genuine concern for her clients. Seasoned buyers and sellers immediately settled down and trusted her, even when she was new to the business. Some said she "had a way with people." Some said she was a "people whisperer."

Joe had learned how to close sales many years ago. He was an excellent judge of weakness or strength in his clients and his competition. He often used this skill for his own good. He believed that each client was fully capable of making up their own minds and certainly intelligent enough to know what to buy or even how to sell. He was the guy that made it all happen for them. He was the closer. Yeah, he might have seen some possible risks for his clients. He might have noticed potential pitfalls. Occasionally he would go as far as pointing them out. But not often. In the end, it was all about the volume for him. He wasn't paid until closing, after all . . . Buying clients were coming out of his ears. Let the good times roll! "Next Up!" was his mantra.

TIP: *Welcome seasoned clients with open arms.*

TRAP: *Some clients may attempt to hijack your job. They fully intend to run the entire process. You must learn the scripts and dialogues that keep you in control of your buyers and sellers.*

When You're Hot, You're Hot!
Get Rich Slowly

GROWING AND THRIVING in this business usually takes special talents and sacrifices. You've learned that by now. Success for you will come one day, for some sooner than others. Welcome the upcoming possibility of less work and more play.

Promise yourself that, when you get a bit of money saved up, you'll invest your money in the one area in which you will gain so much knowledge: real estate. Just think—there are all these fabulous formulas and data to help you make wise choices. There are mathematical models by the hundreds, each designed to make you successful. Don't be fooled into the belief that this stuff is hard to learn. It's not. Don't be scared of the math.

Fact: You won't have to know much more than basic high school math to make millions. All the sophisticated stuff can come later, when you have time to devote to it.

After settling into your successful career as an agent, go buy the books, take the classes, listen to the podcasts. When you feel knowledgeable enough, carve out some time to help investors. Learn by doing. Then you can do for yourself. Below, I list the most influential books I have read on real estate investment:

- *Rich Dad Poor Dad: What the Rich Teach Their Kids About Money That the Poor and Middle Class Do Not!* by Robert Kiyosaki

- *FLIP: How to Find, Fix, and Sell Houses for Profit* by Clay Davis, Gary Keller, and Rick Villan

- *Hold: How to Find, Buy, and Rent Houses for Wealth* by Steve Chader, Jim McKissack, Jennice Doty, and Gary Keller

- *The Book on Rental Property Investing: How to Create Wealth and Passive Income Through Intelligent Buy & Hold Real Estate Investing!* by Brandon Turner

- *How to Invest in Real Estate: The Ultimate Beginner's Guide to Getting Started* by Brandon Turner

- *Real Estate Investment for Dummies* by Eric Tyson and Robert Griswold

- *The Millionaire Real Estate Investor* by Gary Keller, Dave Jenks, and Jay Papasan

- *The ABCs of Real Estate Investing: The Secrets of Finding Hidden Profits Most Investors Miss* by Ken McElroy

I have read and reread each of these. Individually, they bring different ideas and secrets to your future.

Beware: If you "get bit" by the real estate investment bug, remain conservative, buy right, and surround yourself with good people. This is a business you may grow to **love**. You will become as wealthy as you wish.

Then Came the Crash

THE DAY FINALLY CAME. The world economy began to struggle. The national economy began to slowly erode. Interest rates rose dramatically. Joe and Marie's city mirrored the rest of the country. Home buying and selling slowed down to a trickle of what it had been the year before.

Joe's business collapsed. It was like cutting off the water supply. Nobody seemed to want to move to town. The leads he paid for dried up. Housing in his town had frozen in place. He had worked hard, missed family vacations, and spent thousands to become Number One in their city.

Joe's team had grown to six by this time. Slowly, and one by one, each of them left. His past clients remembered him for his lack of patience and short temper. These traits failed to translate in a broken market. Trouble had finally arrived for Joe.

Marie's practice also slowed, but it didn't stop. Gracious and kind, she had stayed in contact with each of her past clients. Her professional relationships seemed fresh and genuine. People continued to get married and have babies. Her families moved around or out of town. They seemed to seek her out almost every time they needed her. Her practice was solid. Clients looked to her for the concern she showed them. They came to her for the truth about the markets. They came to her because they trusted her and knew she would protect them.

The slowdown seemed to drag on and on. The months and years passed, with little to no improvement in the market. Marie and her family kept taking those vacations. She paid for her kids' college tuition. She even replaced that ten-year-old car. Marie realized that real estate investment course she'd taken was about to pay off. Homes were being foreclosed on. Mortgage lenders were forced to discount and liquidate their positions. Foreclosures had risen to all-time highs. Marie and her husband realized this was an ideal time to invest in rental properties. Rental income soon took the place of some of the past sales income. Their net worth was slowly growing and growing. Marie increased her staff to manage their properties. Life was good for Marie and her family.

Closings were few and far between for Joe. All those Internet leads had vanished. Few of his past clients ever really felt they knew Joe. His attitude was brusque; his patience was practically nonexistent. Joe had failed to bond. The result was that few past families chose to call when they needed to sell. Joe's income dropped each month.

Once again (although she did not realize it at the time), it was Joanie to the rescue. She had a few friends at her local bank. Both Joanie and the banker went to Joe and explained that he might want to visit with their work-out specialists. There was plenty of inventory, and the bank had been told by federal regulators they had to get rid of it. This may be a chance for him.

All this repossessing of property (or "repo," as it's known in the industry) appeared foreign to Joe. It seemed a bit below his lofty status. Joe finally agreed to meet up. Joanie explained that he needed to sell something, anything. The bank gave him some listings.

Joe's past sales involved large, expensive, and well-kept homes. When he arrived to inspect his new listings, there were surprises. Lots of surprises.

First of all, many of the foreclosures in his market were modest in size. These were not nearly as large compared to what he was used to selling. The yards were overgrown and lacked maintenance. Pipes were frozen and cracked. Walls were covered with a variety of molds. Roofs were leaky. Critters had taken up residence inside. Every home seemed to have its own acrid smell. Trash and abandoned furniture littered the rooms. Windows were broken. It was truly a culture shock to his system.

Marketing this kind of real estate was not exactly what he had in mind. Joanie turned to her loyal vendors to help with the cleanup. Listings remained on the market for many weeks. Buyers were few and far between, as well as demanding and sophisticated. Pricing had to be continually adjusted. Property owners and banks were forced to cut prices to make deals. They often took a bath on repairs and concessions.

TIP: *It's coming. You may be in one right now—great markets come and great markets go. When there are shifts in markets, they often come quickly. Keep at least six months' living expenses liquid and available at all times.*

TRAP: *Failing to remain vigilant, to remain prepared, may result in panic and missteps for you.*

Joe, Meet Marie.
Marie, Meet Joe!

MARIE AND HER HUSBAND had also made friends at the bank. The work-out specialists had heard that Marie and her husband bought foreclosures. The bank administrators looked forward to working with Marie. They contacted Joe and told him to reach out to Marie and her husband. She made offers through Joe, and the bank accepted them. She bought for pennies on the dollar.

Marie was able to employ her banker, her closing company, her surveyor, her home inspector, her handyman, and her landscaper. The house painter, the flooring people, and the home cleaner were all working for her. She paid each of them promptly. She kept lots of good people employed.

Marie flipped some homes and kept some as rentals. Their profits were modest and consistent. She always looked for win-wins for herself *and* the other side. She was slowly growing rich from the skills she had developed over the years. Her reputation as a true professional had evolved and accelerated. Her vendor base was loyal and responsive. They went out of their way to cut her special concessions.

Over the months, Joe slowly developed a relationship with Marie. Marie and her husband had bought more than a few of Joe's listings. Joe slowly began to warm to Marie's personality and business-like approach. She was a tough customer. She drove a hard bargain. She was a keen judge of home construction and condition. Her knowledge of repair and replacement costs were spot-on. She made decisions to buy or walk away quickly. She always performed on time and on schedule. She kept her word. Joe began to welcome her phone calls. He found himself going out of his way to help her. Marie had helped Joe's practice emerge from its ashes.

The crash continued to melt its way into the market. A few qualified buyers wandered in. Joe found that there were people out there who still had cash money. Investors he had never encountered in the past began to call. These guys were sophisticated and shrewd. Joe was forced to develop an entirely new set of negotiating skills. Slowly, he learned new scripts and dialogues. Other banks in the region heard about Joe. They hired him to liquidate some of their inventory, too. He was finally making some headway.

By now, Joe and Marie had developed a good working relationship. Each had developed a healthy respect for the other. One day during a closing, they both almost said it at the same time. "Let's form a partnership."

A new LLC was born. The new company began by buying homes that went to public auction. Joe did not list these homes, but his contacts inside the industry tipped him off to the upcoming sales. The new small company used some of their own funds and borrowed the rest. Joe learned to work with the attorneys in charge of the auctions. He always got notice of any new inventory coming up. His job was to spot the deals and bring them to his new company. Marie provided the skills needed to figure repairs needed and the costs involved. She also applied her pricing skills to both the purchase side and the sale side of each deal. She worked with their shared vendors to make repairs and upgrades. She also provided the listing and marketing.

Like any residential deals, there were unforeseen problems and issues. The theory was to determine condition, figure the basic costs to make the properties marketable, buy low, make repairs, and sell for a bit higher. It worked. This was turning into real fun!

Make no mistake about it; some days were brutal and exhausting. But overcoming the molehills along with the mountains drew the partners closer. The little company had merged skills, worked through issues respectfully, and become profitable. Survival during the crash had become a bit more profitable and a bit more satisfying.

TIP: *Good fences make good neighbors. Outline all of your business agreements in writing and upfront. Have your attorney oversee your work.*

TRAP: *The wrong people performing a job poorly or not at all may cause small businesses to fail. Don't beat around the bush. Learn when to cut the cord. Sooner is always better than later.*

Chapter 37

Yes, There Is a Light
and an End to the Tunnel

THE DAY IS COMING WHEN WE EACH must finally call it quits. Imagine you are now nearing the end of your career in real estate. You will go out to your last listing and pull up that "For Sale" sign. It's over.

You may take a look back on those years and ask yourself, "How well did I do toward meeting my grand purpose in life? Did I come close to experiencing that dream I had envisioned so long ago? What was the genuine quality of life that my family experienced? In what ways did I impact my clients' lives?"

The economics of retirement now loom on your horizon. Hopefully, early on in your career, you made a few basic plans. You have taken your CPA and financial planners into account and taken action.

Another way to continue your income into retirement is to search out a seasoned agent to partner with. Work out an agreement that pays you well when you refer your past clients.

Further, your real estate agency may offer profit sharing or stock ownership. This is a good thing. This is a very good thing.

Leverage your skill sets and relationships over time. You will learn tough lessons and gain exceptional secrets. Leverage them! You will become an expert in many neighborhoods. Leverage this knowledge! Your fellow agents and your clients will come to you for advice and counsel. You will meet thousands of good people throughout your career who become impressed with you. Leverage them. The wisdom you will accumulate is going to be staggering. Leverage and Capitalize! Form partnerships, brainstorm ideas, look for opportunities to serve. This is perhaps the most satisfying and gratifying part of real estate.

Marie and her husband had made many dear friends over their lifetime. They did not realize it at first, but these loyal clients had told complete strangers about them. Buyers and sellers of investment properties seemed to come out of nowhere. Bit by bit, they accumulated more than a hundred investment properties with no debt. The cash flow at retirement was substantial. Being good guys had paid off for them. They were known as people who always did the right thing. They never seemed to see it that way; good just happened for them.

Joe had joined ranks with Marie during the crash. He had brought his business manager, Joanie, his banking contacts, and his marketing skills. Marie brought her vendors and her relationship-building skills. Together, they bought and flipped houses for many years. Their profits were fairly split. Wisely, they leveraged their profits by investing in tax-advantaged vehicles.

When the time came, they looked back over their careers. Joe and Marie had taken their lumps and found ways to survive the crash. When it got tough, they each reinvented themselves and found ways to serve the slipping housing market. They had lived well below their means, developed rock-solid banking relationships, and bought real estate at bottom dollar. They had become rich very slowly.

Marie's girls had finished university, moved back to the area, and started families of their own. One daughter helped manage the rental properties Marie had accumulated. The other became a loan officer for a mortgage lender. She was like her mom. People grew to love her.

Marie was a grandmother now. She had slowed her practice. Her days were her own now, and there was plenty of time to babysit. Marie had learned to handle the stress of the business. Her meditation, yoga, and workouts had paid off. Marie and her husband traveled all over the world. Life was good.

Following graduate school, Joe's girls chose to live where their jobs took them. Neither were married yet, both pursuing their own professional lives. Joe and his wife went to visit each of them occasionally, and the girls would make it in for Christmas. Travel was not on their radar as much now. Joe had developed heart disease over time, had a pacemaker placed, and hung close to home.

Golf was still his game, and he was very good at it. His group from the club enjoyed the fellowship and competitiveness each time they met. Each and every time he stepped on the course, Joe played to win. He usually did. Sometimes the reward was money, sometimes it was lunch. Life was good.

By now, you have begun to fulfill your "grand purpose" to yourself, your family, and your clients. Your career has been far from perfect, but for all intents and purposes, you've done it and done it well. You are proud of yourself. You learned from your mistakes and brought total and complete defeat to your demons. Congratulations! Look at yourself in the mirror and smile. You have had a wonderful career in service to others and been paid handsomely to do so. BOOM!

Your Very Own Personal Bottom Line

REAL ESTATE IS SIMPLE, but it's anything but easy. Everybody's got to live somewhere, right? Sophisticated software has made it easy to locate the best homes in any city. Buyers from all over the world now view digitally enhanced photos with glowing and descriptive terms. Big changes are on the horizon for real estate. Cities and neighborhoods will be rated by livability, drivability, taxes, education, health stats, crime rate, and other quality-of-life issues.

Artificial intelligence has begun to deliver stunning and powerful information. Analytics will crunch numbers and forecast trends in taxes, interest rates, and even building material costs. Due diligence will include all past history of any home's maintenance, insurance filings, heating and cooling costs, age of roof and mechanicals, and any history of pest infestations. The list will grow each year as more and more data will be accumulated and shared.

Similar to professional athletes, real estate agents will be rated on their overall performance. Reports of our sales volume will likely take a back seat to the quality of client experience that agents deliver.

Successful and unsuccessful client outcomes will become public knowledge. Similar to most things these days, the records will be permanent. Clients will rate us like they do a hotel stay. Stats like "days on the market" or "number of price improvements" will be reported right along with an agent's consistency of communication, attention to detail, ability to solve problems, and market knowledge. Opinions (as most opinions tend to be), will be highly subjective in nature and very powerful.

I submit to you that as human beings, each of us (agent and clients) will continue to exhibit human traits like love, hate, jealousy, insecurity, superiority, egoism, sadness, happiness, pride, and arrogance. Some clients will have a special-needs child or a dying parent. Some clients must win at all costs, while others just want a comfortable place to live. Clients will approach each purchase or sale with their very own emotional and economic needs. Accommodations and compromises will have to be met to close each and every deal. I submit to you that artificial intelligence and the most sophisticated software is a very long way away from participating in this aspect of real estate.

The bottom line is that a skilled, well-trained, empathetic, and street-smart agent must be hired to work out the inevitable issues that arise. It's not about the money for these agents; it's about delivering for their clients. They will gain a reputation for practicing as a professional. The monetary and emotional rewards will show up for the client and the agent. It always does.

Here's what I hope for you and how you will look back at the results of your business and your life.

You learned from the mistakes of others as well as your own. You remained curious. You welcomed changes to your life. You paid the price of long days and nights. Some days and weeks were brutal. You took charge of your business and your life. You persevered. You hung in there. You found a way to win.

You practiced *your own* brand of real estate with wisdom, compassion, patience, and when needed, toughness.

You *always* did the right thing.

Most importantly, you chose to watch out for the best interests of your clients. Through the years, they responded with loyalty and repeat business. Together, you and your clients built a first-class real estate business practice. You made a very comfortable life for yourself and your family. You finished what you came here to do. You attained your Grand Purpose.

About the Author

S TEVE CONDURELIS is a Nashville Tennessee native. He majored in marketing and minored in economics at the University of Tennessee, Knoxville.

He is married to Gaye Givan Condurelis, has a daughter Holly, and has a passion for gardening, trout fishing, and travel.

Education: University of Tennessee,
    B.S. Marketing and Economics 1972
Tennessee Broker license, 1982
GRI, (Graduate Realtors Institute
CRS, Certified Residential Specialist
ABR, (Accredited Buyers Broker)
CRB, (Certified Residential Broker)
Co-owner, Investor, Keller Williams Realty, Nashville, and Franklin, Tn.
Experience: Residential Sales and Listings, 1988-present
Life-Time Award Sales, Greater Nashville Realtors Association
Greater Nashville Realtors Association, Board of Directors (retired)

Chairman Professional Standards, Greater Nashville Realtors Association (retired)

Instructor: listing specialist, buyer representation, new home construction, flip and home renovations, Investment Real Estate, and retirement planning.

Entrepreneur: Steve has started successful businesses in six separate industries, health and wellness, building maintenance, real estate development, House flipping and resale, ownership and management of investment properties, and residential brokerage ownership.